T0358203

# CHINA FOR
# SMEs
## Essential Elements
## of Success

# CHINA FOR
# SMEs
## Essential Elements
## of Success

**Daryl Guppy**

Guppytraders.com

 **World Scientific**

NEW JERSEY · LONDON · SINGAPORE · BEIJING · SHANGHAI · HONG KONG · TAIPEI · CHENNAI · TOKYO

*Published by*

World Scientific Publishing Co. Pte. Ltd.
5 Toh Tuck Link, Singapore 596224
*USA office:* 27 Warren Street, Suite 401-402, Hackensack, NJ 07601
*UK office:* 57 Shelton Street, Covent Garden, London WC2H 9HE

**Library of Congress Cataloging-in-Publication Data**
Names: Guppy, Daryl J., 1954–   author.
Title: China for SMEs : essential elements of success / Daryl Guppy.
Description: New Jersey : World Scientific, [2021]
Identifiers: LCCN 2020054697 | ISBN 9789811232510 (hardcover) |
    ISBN 9789811233845 (paperback) | ISBN 9789811232527 (ebook) |
    ISBN 9789811232534 (ebook other)
Subjects: LCSH: Yi dai yi lu (Initiative : China) | Business enterprises, Foreign--China. |
    Investments, Foreign--China. | Small business--China. | Business etiquette--China. |
    China--Commerce. | China--Foreign economic relations. | China--Economic policy--2000–
Classification: LCC HF3834 .G87 2021 | DDC 330.951--dc23
LC record available at https://lccn.loc.gov/2020054697

**British Library Cataloguing-in-Publication Data**
A catalogue record for this book is available from the British Library.

For any available supplementary material, please visit
https://www.worldscientific.com/worldscibooks/10.1142/12167#t=suppl

Desk Editor: Lixi Dong

Typeset by Stallion Press
Email: enquiries@stallionpress.com

Printed in Singapore

# ENDORSEMENTS

Many of the nuances that drive Chinese human behaviour have been thousands of years in the making. The prospects of foreigners doing business successfully in China are greatly enhanced by a respect for, and appreciation of, these quirks of Chinese behaviour. Daryl Guppy's book is a rich repository of such behavioural observations, nuances and understandings which are fundamental to building the all-important relationships and trust that drive successful engagement with the Chinese. This is a book written with the small to medium business person in mind. However, anyone looking to engage successfully with the Chinese would benefit greatly from exploring the insights which shape the "deep seated" perceptions of the Chinese people.

*Hon. Andrew Robb AO*
*Former Minister for Trade and Investment and architect of the China Australia Free Trade Agreement.*

If you want to do business in China, this book is an absolute must. Nobody I know understands China and the Chinese people as well as Daryl Guppy. His knowledge and insights are built on his decades of business experience, his wide networks and friendships and his fluency in Mandarin. His book is entertaining and very readable — but above all, masterful in identifying the "must knows" and "must do's" in undertaking business in China. With the world's biggest economy in purchasing power parity terms, China continues to drive global economic growth and new business opportunities. I strongly recommend this book for anyone currently doing business, studying business or wanting to do business with China.

**John Brumby**
*Former Premier of Victoria, Australia and National President of the Australia China Business Council 2014–2019.*

Drawing on his twenty years of hands-on, personal, experience, Daryl Guppy has distilled a lifetime of lessons — great disappointments and successes — into a guide for new and even existing SME participants in the China market. Guppy carefully analyses how to win, or as in his concluding chapter, "to be the one". Guppy's great skill is to eschew the usual cliches and urban myths about doing business in China. Instead, he emphasises the background work required to know your customer, know your market, know the diversity of China, even within a single city, know yourself, and know your offer, be it in products or services. The challenges are great but so are the potential rewards if done properly. Guppy's analysis will help many to get to success for years to come.

**Geoff Raby**
*Former Australian Ambassador to China, Independent ASX company director, Chairman, Geoff Raby and Associates. His latest book, **China's Grand Strategy and Australia's Future in the New Global Order** has been published by Melbourne UP, in November 2020.*

Daryl Guppy takes SMEs out of the classroom and into the real world of doing business in China. A refreshingly practical guide to navigating the path to business success in China. A must-read for every SME with aspirations for success in the China market. Refreshingly free of business school jargon.

**Michael Clifton**
*Former Head of the Australian Trade and Investment Commission's network across Greater China in Beijing, Shanghai and Hong Kong*

There is a big difference between doing business in China and doing business in China _successfully_. Daryl Guppy's book is right on point as it draws on his extensive experience working in China. You'll learn that running a successful business in China is possible, as long as you have the right tools for the job: fundamental knowledge — a deep understanding — passion and, most importantly, patience. Daryl gives necessary insights and so much more. This is a must-read for any SME wanting to enter this exciting market or improve their current market position. Light-hearted at times but always interesting and educational. Essential reading if you want to enter the den of the Dragon.

**_Willem Westra van Holthe_**
_Former Northern Territory Minister for Mines and Energy_

Daryl Guppy provides vivid and realistic descriptions of many practical situations that business people face in China. These range from introductions and meeting protocols and nuances in negotiation through to the emergence of transformational digital platforms such as WeChat. Guppy's many years of experience doing business in China shine through as he weaves into the book countless useful snippets, or bites, as he calls them, of information and insight into the cultural setting for business in China, including the different roles that relationships can play when doing business in China. Guppy helps the reader understand the speed and extent of change in China and assesses the potential for China's Belt and Road Initiative and its other international economic and financial policies to create new challenges and opportunities for foreign companies. _China for SMEs_ is full of clear, sometimes provocative, assessments and is a very easy to read introduction to doing business in China.

**_Laurie Smith_**
_Former Executive Director, International Operations, Australian Trade Commission and former Regional Director, North East Asia, Australian Trade Commission_

In 2016, as the then Minister for Mines and Energy, I led, with a lot of optimism and a feeling that we would do really well there, a delegation of officials and mining executives to China to promote the Northern Territory's mining potential. We all knew the cliches about China's appetite for mineral resources, the huge number of clients and a big market with not much competition in our field. In that trip we achieved very little! It was only when we accepted that we had to learn about and act the Chinese way that we started making progress in China. We learned that you had to study China and its provinces, to create relationships and networks in China, socialise and spend time knowing your potential clients before you could even start promoting your products. I wish I could have read Daryl Guppy's book about China first before our trip there. Finally we learnt the hard way but Daryl's book puts all these information together, making it easier and quicker to understand and do business in China.

**Kon Vatskalis**
*Lord Mayor of Darwin and former Northern Territory Minister for Mines and Energy*

This book is not only instructive for those who wish to do business in China, but also enlightening for the local businesses in China who are prepared to engage with foreign partners. As the philosopher Wang Yangming from the Ming Dynasty says, "Knowledge and action are one". *China for SMEs* is the author's years of "knowing" and "doing" in China and the Chinese communities worldwide. Reliable, informative, and interesting.

**Emma Wei (Ms.)**
*Director of Membership Center, Silk Road Chamber of International Commerce, Beijing*

# FOREWORD

October is a special time in China — a celebration of culture, a national holiday and traditional gifting to friends, family and business acquaintances — many mooncake gifts flow across the nation and the globe. I write this introduction on the anniversary of this National Day of the People's Republic of China, a day of symbolic commemoration and significance to many people across the world. The Golden Week of celebrations.

This wonderfully insightful book by Daryl Guppy illustrates the deep culture of China and its pervading influence on today. There is the strength of Chinese history, the nation's pride in that history and culture that is today reflected in China's approach, globally and domestically, to business and more broadly, relationships. China has a renewed pride in its economic progress which has been astounding.

With the emergence of China as a global market player, there is much to know if businesses small and large are to enter the market successfully and be able to achieve sustainable success.

This book helps with carefully thought out strategies and illuminates understandings which are invaluable to success.

Daryl Guppy transits the many aspects of China, its sheer size geographically, its many challenges of rapid urban growth and the nuance required to achieve business outcomes, the value of patience in building trust and the need for reciprocal respect in addition to the need of a considered partner selection and maintenance.

This is more than a practical guide. This is wisdom collected over many years impacted with sincerity and style, wrapped in anecdotal observations that are lessons to be absorbed and to be contemplated upon.

This is a fine book and a refreshing optimistic approach to the phenomenon that is China in our world — a changing China we must understand in all its manifestation.

The keen business person will find so much in this book and it is a very worthy and successful presentation from one of Australia's foremost and successful business participants in China over the last 30 years.

### *The Hon. Warwick L. Smith AO*

*Former Minister of Territories and often visitor to Northern Territory in that role and many other roles in government and business over the past 35 years. Former Chairman of the Australia China Council and inaugural Chairman of The National Foundation of Australia China Relations.*

# CONTENTS

# Introduction

# China Business Bites

A Chinese banquet consists of many small dishes and guests are expected to take many small bites. The combination of small and diverse flavours makes up the overall impression of the meal and influence your lasting impressions. This book takes the same approach, bringing together small bites to build a larger banquet of China experience. More importantly, this book reveals the secret ingredients that make a good dish exceptional. These are the herb and spice combinations to turn business in China into true success.

This is not a comprehensive and exhaustive how-to book on China business. There are plenty of those around. This book covers the observations of the things not included in these strategic overviews. These are the small bites, the little things, the quirks of Chinese behaviour, and knowing these gives you an edge in China because they put you in tune with the deep- seated perceptions of the Chinese people you are dealing with.

I have included a section on the Belt and Road Initiative because this is the new foundation environment of business and China and investment coming out of China. This is a larger bite and you may find it indigestible because it's different to the perspectives dominating Western media coverage of the Belt and Road. We make no apologies for its inclusion in the banquet because failure to understand this environment makes China business so much more difficult.

This book is not designed for the big corporates working in China. Their staff are the faces of global companies and have the backing of conglomerates. This book gives you the information you need when business is smaller and tougher. It's for the small and medium enterprises where you, the CEO, have to personally undertake the hard work to break into this market. It's for those businesses where success or failure sits on the shoulders of a small group of people, often working with limited support. This is the book for those who dare to dream about China business.

Address an envelope in China and you start from the big and go to the small. At a China post office, I would send a letter to Liaoning Province, Dalian City, suburb, building, floor number and apartment and finally family name and name, Yang, Jin Zhao. At a Western post office, I would send it to Jin Zhao Yang, apartment number, floor, building, suburb, Dalian, Liaoning Province. It's a different view of the world and our place in it. In this book we use the China approach, working from the large to the small. In the first section on business we take a brief look at some of the larger issues before moving quickly down to the smaller business bites.

In America and the West there is a foundation belief that everybody is born equal. The backwoodsman can become US president. Every aging actor can aspire to leadership and multiple business failures are no barriers to presidential success. Every idea, good or bad, has the equal opportunity to grow up and become national policy.

In China this idea makes no sense because the Chinese believe everybody is born connected. The unfortunates are those who are not connected. Success depends upon connections, and the word is used in a much broader sense than this Western translation.

Understanding this difference is the first critical foundation of success in China business. This book cannot give you the connections, but I can show you how these connections work in everyday meals, meetings and friendships.

Relationship is the one word repeated over and over again throughout these chapters. Relationships are the very oxygen that gives all life in China and there is no avoiding this repetition. The application of law in China is not always consistent. Much is left to interpretation by local officials. A consequence of this is a greater reliance on relationships for building long term business. Trust is essential when law is malleable.

You cannot buy relationships, but you will need to spend time and sincere effort to develop these relationships from ground zero because you were not born connected.

The Chinese are by necessity more shrewd in divining the true feelings you bring to the table and the business table. If it's just money you want then you will get a deal structured on that basis and miss out on so many more opportunities that develop from business based on friendship and trust. Trust is not easily given, and it may be frequently and deliberately tested. It's a process of confirmation and reassurance just as a haulier will stop frequently to retest the ropes holding down his load.

With true Daoist duality, the very strength of your business in China is also the most vulnerable point of weakness. This book will show how all successful China business is built on relationships in a way that is not the case in the West. However, what happens when the person you have developed a good relationship with is promoted, transferred, or retires? The foundation of your business lurches because there is no systemic structure supporting it. This is the key danger in relationship-based business. It's overcome by developing a wider network of relationships and not just relying on a single individual, or small group.

I have advised governments and businesses on their China business and investment attraction strategies. I sit on the board of the Australia China Business Council and I have advised European, Singaporean, and Malaysian Chinese businesses on better approaches to working in China. In another book I authored, *The 36 Strategies of the Chinese for Financial Traders,* I bring together Chinese philosophy and modern financial markets.

In this book I draw on my deep experience working in China from a SME perspective. I draw on my work with the Silk Road Chambers of International Commerce and ASEAN and APEC forums in China. I draw on my experience in writing regular columns for Chinese newspapers, including China Daily, Shanghai Security News and China Global Television Network Digital. From all of this I offer you a banquet of ideas to improve your understanding of China and of China business.

Our company website www.workingwithChina.com collates a number of training, teaching and consultancy modules we use to assist with business development and strategic planning in China. Some of the case studies in this book draw on these programs.

The first section looks at business and concludes with two case studies encompassing common frustrations, and more importantly, solutions. This section is not the grand strategic approach to developing a global market presence in China. It's more properly a second course rather than dim sum starters but we cater to the Western habit of skipping the entrée and moving straight on to the mains. We look at how easy it is to get it wrong and also how easy it is, with just a twist, to get it right. These are the aptitudes we have found most useful in developing solid foundations for China business when you are alone in the Chinese economic landscape. It's an exercise in managing expectations and it gives us the opportunity to move on to a more sympathetic appreciation of the Chinese people we work with. These dim sum bites are out of order in the grand plan of banquet servings, but we think they are more palatable in this sequence.

The second section examines the evolving Belt and Road Initiative (BRI). It started life as the New Silk Road before becoming One Belt One Road and then morphed into the Belt and Road Initiative. This is a foundation policy that underpins almost all business activity in China. Often portrayed in Western media as a security threat, the BRI is a trade framework. Structuring investment and business proposals within this BRI policy framework speeds up the approvals process, particularly where foreign currency transfers are required. We examine the broader concepts of BRI so you can make a more informed decision about how to integrate this into your China business engagement.

The third section is about people. It's a bite here and a bite there, dipping into behaviours and attitudes which sprinkle every business relationship in China. Working with the Chinese can be one of the most rewarding and also the most frustrating of experiences. It is difficult to comprehend just how different the starting point may be. The point where you and your Chinese partners intersect has commonalities of interest but your respective starting points on the roads leading to this point of intersection, this meeting, are very different. This diverse mix of expectations, of beliefs, of practices create the potential for monumental levels of confusion. This can rapidly escalate from the quaintly amusing to the very serious.

This is a complex area and the experiences we include are just a small sample. Use these as an example of how to recognise when there is a problem before it becomes too large to ignore. Use this section for some guide on how to resolve these differences in perception and work with them rather than against them. Much of this revolves around eating. In the West we see this as a necessary fuel for existence — we eat to live. In China, eating is the necessary fuel for life — they live to eat. The layers of complexity in a Chinese lunch reflects the levels of complexity in personal relationships in this cross-cultural environment. Getting the details right is not the same as understanding why the details must be as they are. Two case studies encapsulate solutions.

It's usually at this point in time that many people throw up their hands in horror, exclaiming that it's all so Chinese and much too difficult. This is not a point of capitulation. It's a point of celebration because it shows you understand there are significant differences that go beyond the quaint and exotic.

The fourth section is the point where some people choose to walk away. Others glimpse the far horizon and start to explore what they really need to know to grow a long term sustainable and profitable business with China. It's a significant change in attitude and approach, but some of our intuitive directions are not quite as relevant as we expect. There remains ample room for mistakes, confusion, frustration and for lots of fun as the Chinese recognise your commitment and extend a helping hand. This is the stage where snapshots don't capture the true flavour of where you are and what you need to do. This gives you the confidence to leave the hotel by yourself, move confidently outside of areas dominated by Westerners and Western tourists and test the boundaries of your language. This is where you stop just bringing back photos of your time in China and start to bring back ideas.

The fifth section explores a few of the myths surrounding our China experience. These are a complex mixture of modern fallacies, ancient embroideries, and base level perceptions grounded in propaganda from the 1830s and still reinforced by Hollywood and popular fiction a century or more later. On one level it makes for disappointing reading because our understanding has advanced so little. On another level it takes us forward because we recognise and acknowledge the role these myths have played in shaping our public and personal perceptions of China. Finding them, identifying them, and throwing them out are essential steps to creating and doing better business in China.

No life is lived on an island and my introduction to China involves more friends and unwitting helpers in taxi drivers, restaurants and hotel staff than I can acknowledge. Pivotal in my China education is my very good friend and colleague, Chen Jing. My learning is just a fraction of her unparalleled skill and knowledge and I have tried her patience as a teacher many times. From the top of Mount Tai Shan to the slopes of Xiang Shan mountain in Beijing we share great times. My dear friend Yang Nannan taught me much more than she realises. My friend and colleague Emma Wei, Executive Director of the Silk Road Chambers of International Commerce has been essential in opening up my understanding of the broader world of the BRI. My friend Lisa O'Donoghue and I have worked together and she shares her experience of bringing Chinese investors to a foreign country. My wife Marion has accompanied me through the production of yet another book with patience and endurance. I treasure all these individuals as *zhi you* 挚友 — true friends acquired by the beneficent hand of *yuan fen* 缘份 — for which 'fate' is an inadequate translation.

At the end of the Han Dynasty in 208 AD, two skilled generals, Liu Bei and Sun Quan, formed an allied force with a smaller troop of soldiers to fight against the seemingly more superior army led by warlord Cao Cao. The battle of *Chi bi* 赤壁 Red Cliff was fought on the banks of the Yangtze River in Hubei province. The decisive attack using a fleet of fire ships against Cao Cao's untrained naval forces was skilfully timed and launched by the allied forces when the east wind blew in their favour. Wait for the East Wind — *wan shi ju bei, zhi qian dong feng* 万事俱备, 只欠东风 is a Chinese metaphor for understanding the operating environment, preparing carefully for tactical execution, and finally achieving decisive victory despite overwhelming odds. It is a good description of the circumstances many Western businesses must create if they are to succeed in China.

This book is a banquet. It brings together some of the lessons I have drawn from working in China but my education is far from complete. Treat these as student notes passed to other students rather than as notes from the professor at the front of room. Work long enough in China and you will understand this perspective. These bites are based on experience and observation. They will not suit every situation but this information gives you a starting point to advance more smoothly into this challenging and irresistible environment. Get your China strategy wrong and China business will bite you.

China is not for the faint-hearted. You either like it, or hate it. There is no room for indifference but ample room for compromise.

Daryl Guppy
Beijing, Singapore, Darwin
2021

## Acknowledgement

Parts of chapters 11, 18, 33 and 36 were first published in TerritoryQ. Parts of chapters 15, 16, 17 and 19 were first published by CGTN Digital.

# Chapter 1

# THE CHINA SYNDROME

It is getting too cold for tourists in Xi'an and the visitation pressure comes off the terracotta warriors. The cold doesn't stop the nighty flood of visitors to the Great Tang Mall stretching south from the Big Wild Goose pagoda where the first Buddhist scripture in China were translated for the Tang dynasty court. The mall stretches over two city blocks and is dominated by stately statues of past emperors and the Tang poets like Li Bai and Du Fu.

Unashamedly designed for tourists it also captures a Chinese cultural outlook. In mid-December the throngs of Xi'an residents, free from tourists, provide some ongoing perspectives which are easily overlooked by visitors.

This night, at the southern end of the mall, the truly giant LED screen is showing what many foreigners would class as a propaganda clip. It extols the virtues of Xi'an and the progress being made as a terminus of both the ancient and the new silk road. It's outright publicity for the inland rail port and the free trade zone. It's a lengthy clip that Westerners in particular would not watch voluntarily.

And yet this clip attracts a significantly large crowd. This type of advertising — propaganda, as its often translated from Chinese — is a legacy from the time when illiteracy levels were high. The new Maoist Government in particular became skilled at using graphic images to deliver its messages of reform, progress and revolution. This advertising propaganda tradition continues, and it continues to fill its role of informing people.

But make no mistake, there is a genuine quiet pride in the achievements being shown on screen. When doing business in China we will do well to remember these deep running sentiments.

Evident too is an increasing pride in Chinese history and traditions. Perhaps it is more evident along the Tang mall because Xi'an, once known as Chang'an, was the capital of the Tang Dynasty which rivalled the wealth and sophistication of any Italian renaissance cities.

The crowd is dotted with many young and not so young women wearing traditional Han dresses and cloaks with modern sneakers poking out below the hem of long dresses. These are hired costumes and it's a hire business that does well with four shops specialising not just in clothing, but hairstyles and jewellery accessories. Often the young women are accompanied by their boyfriends, also dressed in Tang Dynasty style. They pause, sipping coke, or snacking on Grandpa Li's steamed rice cakes, as they watch a classical violin quartet, a modern K-pop singer, or listen to a Mongolian group playing a morin khuur — Horse Head fiddle — and singing the Beach Boys classic *Kokomo* in Mandarin whilst the first flakes of snow drift in the cold wind.

This is a celebration of China, but it is not a nationalism that demands others should emulate China. It is a celebration of pride and a statement of respect deserved and delivered. The days when something foreign automatically commanded status are long past. The new status labels read "Designed and made in China — with pride." This is a changed marketplace, with change accelerated by trade wars. It is an unintended consequence and those wanting to do business in China need to take notice because the China Syndrome can blind them to reality.

The China Syndrome is a dangerous infection often leading to financial ruin. Consider an eager potential business exporter to China. He is a middle scale entrepreneur, running a successful SME business and looking to expand the reach of his services and products. He exhibits all the signs of the China Syndrome with a collection of untested personal beliefs about China and the business opportunities offered.

Here are some of the symptoms:

- China has billions of customers so I only need to get a very very small fraction to make a fortune with my business.
- China is a competition desert so there is room for my advanced product or service. The emerging middle class is hungry for my product.
- China is desperate for foreign knowledge and expertise to replace their outdated thinking.
- Apart from the language, China is pretty similar to working in any other Asian country with a large Chinese population like Singapore.

Let's examine these beliefs one at a time.

The idea that China has billions of customers is a modern variation on the Shanghai Tailors' dream. This was a dream of British cotton merchants fuelled by wild back-of-the- envelope calculations over a gin and tonic at the bar in the Cathay Hotel, now the Peace Hotel, on Nanjing East road near the Shanghai bund. They calculated that if every Chinese added just an inch to their shirt tails then all the merchants would enjoy untold wealth beyond imagination. It was such a small request with such massive potential.

There are millions of potential customers in China but getting them to buy your product or service requires a lot of research and effort. Add to this the costs of doing business in overseas markets and the challenges are substantial. It takes as much effort, if not more, to gather Chinese customers as it does to gather customers in your home country.

It is true a city like Beijing offers a potential customer base of about the same population size of a country like Australia. Reaching those customers is more difficult because of language, logistics, expectations, consumer spending habits and product or service suitability. It is worth trying, but only if your expectations are realistic.

China is not a competition desert. For every product and service you can think of, there are established local competitors already in China.

You need to compete on price, on service, or brand status. It is highly unlikely your product or service will fill a previously undiscovered gap in the market.

The Chinese market is sophisticated and well developed. This is not an emerging market like Vietnam with poorly developed and unexploited market segments. China has emerged and is now, by many measures, the world's largest economy. It is foolish to think there are business and service niches that are not already filled. Your product or service has to compete against other businesses which have the advantage of local knowledge.

Your lack of knowledge about the true situation in China is not an excuse for wishful thinking. China is not a soft option for exports.

There is a large and expanding middle class and this is changing many consumer habits. This ranges from an increased demand for meat to creating the world's largest market for high end luxury goods delivered in a sophisticated e-commerce and increasingly cashless environment. So where does your product or service fit into the rankings on a world scale? If it's not globally competitive then it will not be competitive or attractive to the emerging middle class in China.

China is not an export market for second rate services or products. Success requires world class standards and not just measured against the standards in your home market. Chinese standards of e-commerce, 5G, blockchain and Artificial Intelligence are the advanced global standards you will need to meet. The wider availability of labour delivers higher service standards than you are probably accustomed to.

IKEA in China provides service personnel to go to your home and assemble the box of wood and screws that you purchased. No left-over fasteners, no wood panels assembled inside-out and an end product that looks exactly like the photo in the catalogue. That's service in China and it's a standard you need to compete against.

This is not to say the days of rude, abusive and contemptuous service have disappeared in China. You do not need to travel to the countryside or to second tier cities to find good examples of this but the survival of small Chinese companies is not your concern. Your survival depends on better service standards because your product is most likely more expensive in an already crowded marketplace. The value-add requires more than just the prestige of a foreign brand name.

There was a time, perhaps thirty or more years ago, when China was desperate for foreign knowledge and experience. This has changed and the foreign premium has shrunk. The 15% margin or more for foreign products has been sliced to razor thin margins. The shrinking status of foreigners is reflected in a raft of new laws that erode expat benefits.

China remains interested in new ideas, but it is even more interested in how those ideas can be applied in a local environment and adjusted to be compatible with Chinese methods and approaches. China is not interested in blindly adopting foreign ideas and behaviours and nor do they regard their thinking as outdated. These are assumptions of Western cultural superiority. They are misplaced and bad for business.

The differences in China go well beyond language. China is vastly different from any other country. This is a function of continuous history and size. Ordinary people standing in front of an ancient stele at a Buddhist monastery can read many of the characters inscribed in the stone. Unless your grasp of schoolboy Latin is excellent, this is not something you can do when you stand in front of similar commemorative stele in Rome. This gives Chinese people a direct connection with history where the 14th century novel, the *Romance of The Three Kingdoms* is as real and recent and relevant as today's latest film.

The contrasts between large city, small city and countryside are not just about size. These differences permeate the supply chain, the logistics system, the way of doing business and business relationships. Business may be a universal language, but it has many different dialects. The skills and experience learned in business in your home country cannot be easily or directly transferred to doing business in China.

Fortunately, the China Syndrome can be cured and the remaining chapters will explain some of the methods.

## CHINA BUSINESS BITE

China is a sophisticated, developed market. It is as challenging to break into as a Western market. With additional complications created by cultural differences, the Chinese business story is a significant challenge. Get this wrong and China will bite back.

# Chapter 2

# CHINA CHAMPIONS

You are geared up to expand your business into China. It's a great idea, but what drives your China strategy? It is a question I was forced to ask when working with a Singapore company board; the process is relevant for every company operating in or aspiring to operate in China.

The China business unit in the company was effective. The small team had developed a good track record of success in developing and sustaining China business. In addition, it also had a formidable reservoir of intellectual property and expertise in relation to event organisation, sponsorship and management. Better still, the team's recent work had been profitable, and the profits were sufficient to cover losses incurred in the early stages of the business development. The unit was in the black and contributing income to the company.

Yet the mood in the team was depressed. Despite their best efforts, the momentum had gone out of the China strategy at a company level. China had become just one part of the company's domestic and international strategy. A change in the structure of the management board had seen the removal of a China champion. This person had been headhunted by another China orientated organisation.

The China champion believed passionately in the potential of the China market. He wasn't particularly skilled in terms of understanding Chinese business culture but he was convinced the company had to be in China and that it had to develop long-term business in China. Armed with an idea and a conviction, he set out to assemble a team of skilled managers and staff who could deliver on his vision. This was China strategy driven from the top.

The team he put together, and the team he empowered, had the skills, the knowledge and the experience to fill in the gaps and the details within the framework of the broader China strategy. In board meetings the China champion fought for his team, not just because they were good, but because he believed in the importance of what they were doing. He fought for the idea of China as a significant business opportunity.

When he left the company, he did not take any particular China-specific skills or knowledge with him. The China team he had developed remained behind. But when he left, dedication, commitment and belief in the China strategy also left the board room. Regrettably, the likelihood of failure for the company's China strategy then increased, because China business is a hard road. The nuances and demands of operating in China are not just different, they are very different.

Doing China business well is very hard work. Doing China business with consistent success on a long-term basis is exceptionally hard work. It requires a commitment to the idea rather than just working long hours and under high pressure. Unless the top levels of company management and the board share this commitment, then there is a tendency to treat China business as much the same as business in other countries.

All of the evidence of success, and of failure of China enterprises, suggests business in China is not much the same as business in other countries. Later on, we will look at some of the specific nuances of China business, including hosting expectations, operational differences and Chinese perceptions that place obstacles in the way of smooth operations. For now, it is sufficient to note that it is the reservoir of hard-won experience in just getting to the place where deals can be done that determines the long-term success of China business.

Working in China is the difference between playing two-dimensional chess which is an adequate metaphor for Western business development, and playing three-dimensional chess which is a more accurate description of China business development. They may look similar, but the similarity obscures profound differences in the way the game is played.

Within eight weeks most of the China team in the Singapore company had left. They found work with several different companies. The best of the team is working with companies that have China champions at management level. They will carve out new business opportunities with China for their employers because they understand the subtlety of China business. The old company the team left found that their China business stalled at first. Then the business slid backwards because China business requires high and detailed maintenance.

China teams do not have to be Chinese. Most times they are drawn from Westerners already working in the company. Some may have the ability to speak Chinese but this should not be confused with the ability to understand Chinese. The difference is critical because understanding what is meant rather than just what is said is the foundation of smooth business development.

The China business teams in Western countries often include some China staff from first generation immigrants, such as Singapore, Taiwan or Hong Kong. If you are lucky, the team may include PRC (People's Republic of China) staff from the mainland. Staff with most potential value for the China team are naturally PRC-born because they understand the current mainland environment. You would not expect an English-speaking Irishman fresh from Ireland to understand the nuances of business conditions in America just because he can speak English, but all too often we expect a Chinese-speaking Singaporean to understand the business conditions in Beijing simply because he can speak Chinese.

Increasingly companies with Chinese aspirations are employing PRC staff. However, it not clear that they always make the best use of staff. All too often, PRC China staff are a token gesture and their contribution to fast tracking China business is ignored.

There are five levels of PRC staff deployment.

1) Foreign workers in the office who are employed for their office skills and who just happen to have a second language. Their employment

is used as evidence of support for cultural diversity in the workplace or as support for the company's China friendly image. Little thought is given to what these staff can offer beyond their formal qualifications.

2) Chinese-speaking staff are deployed on a casual basis for translation tasks. This includes checking the translation of some documents, or helping with short translation tasks. Staff are mainly employed for their other office skills, and their second language and translation ability is treated as a cost saving bonus.

3) Chinese staff provide advice on Western business operations in China. This often involves the translation and interpretation of new Chinese rules and regulations. It may involve the translations of documents, or the checking of documents translated by an outside service.

The core of this work is advanced translation and reading skills. All too often this is seen as evidence of strong China engagement. Much of their work is the facilitation of Western business practices where they intersect with Chinese regulatory requirements.

The reverse applies when this type of advice is delivered to Chinese companies in your home country and is the equivalent of a Chinese translation of Western business regulations.

These are essential functions for both Western and Chinese businesses but they do not get to the core of building business through genuine understanding. Reading between the lines is difficult. Reading between the characters is a difficulty of a much higher order.

4) Chinese staff provide information and support about the culture of business in China. This is part of how the company can do business in China. There is some translation and interpretation work but the main focus is on explaining to the Western company managers the problems of doing business in China. They pay the role of middleman between Western concepts and the often bewildering Chinese business concepts. This is the mechanics of business, but not an understanding of business on both sides.

All too often this is a one-way engagement with China aimed at working through and around problems without understanding why these problems may have occurred. This type of service may also be provided by a Western China expert. When it is provided by Chinese staff, it is often seen as a cost saving because it keeps costs in-house. It's actually a mistake to treat these staff as a type of in-house consultant. The narrow perspective means the company fails to fully utilise their skill and knowledge.

5) At this ultimate level the Chinese staff interpret and explain the practices of business in China and the way these interact with business in your home country. This is a two-way flow. These staff provide a bridge between the two business cultures, explaining Western business practices to their Chinese counterparts and Chinese business practices to the Western office. The work involved at this level is to explain and understand the different drivers of business practice in China and the home country, so co-operative solutions can be created. These staff become the China champion team in a business, working alongside Western partners to advise them on protocol both when they visit China and when Chinese counterparts visit their office. On a broader level, this is one of the roles filled by the best of China consultants who draw on a knowledge of why things are done, as well as how things are done from both perspectives.

Chinese staff provide a reservoir of skills and knowledge about working with China that is all too often underutilised in the company. It is certainly a mistake to assume every Chinese will have a good knowledge of business practices, but it is also a mistake to use these staff at lower translation levels when they have a wider range of skills appropriate for Chinese business. They might not fully understand the company strategy, but they can tell you a meal with Chinese counterparts is not just about obligatory socialising. They can point to the different undercurrents running through a meal and its arrangements. They can explain the expectations of a Chinese delegation so you understand why an environmentally friendly calico conference goodie bag is not appropriate. Unfortunately, these staff skills are all too often ignored simply because managers fail to ask the right questions or recognise the depth of experience and talent they have in their Chinese staff.

Not everyone is confident or competent in these areas, but unless you ask, or give staff the opportunity, then you will never know just how much competence you have in-house. When Chinese staff are used for translation, take the time to ask for their opinion and assessment. Their answers might be particularly useful.

When organising or hosting an event for a Chinese delegation, don't make the assumption that you already have all the answers because you have organised events for other Western delegations visiting China. A conversation with Chinese staff may point the way to some things of particular importance to your guests that you have overlooked, or considered to be unimportant.

China literate companies mean much more than just having Chinese-speaking staff and employing a number of Chinese people in the office. Aside from the formal technical job they are doing, Chinese staff provide a reservoir of everyday China skills and experience which they are more than willing to share if they are asked and if they feel their answers are listened to. For companies doing business in China, their Western-based Chinese staff should be much more than a convenient, even if high level, substitute for Google translate.

What drives your China strategy? It must be China from the top. Anything less is a waste of time. China champions come from management and from staff. They are the foundation of your China strategy but they are usually operating from an office outside of China.

You can dip your toes in the water and develop business in China from your office in your home country but at some stage you will need to step more fully into the China business environment.

Having an office presence in China is essential if you want to do genuine business in China. Your Chinese customers like to deal with a local presence and prefer to deal with native language speakers. They also want to do this for the cost of a local call and within their own time zone. Companies need to set up either a serviced or virtual office in China to deal with client and customer enquiries, and establish a 'face' office presence in China.

A virtual office allows you to leverage a network of services and solutions without having to maintain a physical office. It provides everything you need to run your business professionally, effectively and without the costly overheads. Typically, a virtual office includes a prestigious address, a local business telephone number and a dedicated receptionist managing your calls at your chosen location. For any caller it sounds like it is your office but the limitation is that clients cannot visit and meet your staff.

Usually the virtual office concept also offers access to boardrooms, meeting rooms and day offices on an as-needed basis. Access to videoconferencing and online meeting hosting, mail and courier management may also be included.

A serviced office allows you to run your business from a CBD address. This includes access to secretarial team support and IT infrastructure without incurring the costs and financial commitment of long-term leasing and staffing. It provides a foundation for expansion, with additional services available until you reach the critical stage of development where it makes sense to open your own office with company staff.

A serviced office usually includes a dedicated receptionist, professional meeting rooms with secretarial support on hand. Payment is usually on a flexible month-by-month basis. The serviced office concept gives the business access to an office address, usually well located in the CBD, and a local telephone number. The serviced office also provides dedicated staff who will answer the phone in your name, but using the local language. Depending on the service level you select, this can be simply a message taking and relay service, or a limited product information line. Other services include translation of documents, use of office space, arranging interpreters and translators and a mail drop delivery point.

The one stop solution of such virtual or serviced offices allows companies new to China to focus on core business activities because they can bypass the problems of finding an office, employing staff and dealing with the maze of regulations in this area. This is an effective way of developing an office presence with a prestigious address. It also allows companies to avoid the multitude of problems associated with leasing office space in China.

The serviced office options provide an effective way to move into the China market without costly overheads and massive budgets. They have a downside. Chinese are suspicious of *shou ti bao gong si* 手提包 公司 — handbag companies. These are the equivalent of the carpet bag companies that littered the American West in the 19th century.

Getting a good address gives a company 'face'. It is the first step in learning how to do business China style. Developing the confidence for a lasting business relationship that goes beyond just the exchange of money is the essence of China business. It is impossible to make any progress beyond dreaming and scheming unless you have an understanding of 'face'. This is more complex than we imagine in the West and any Western explanation must always be incomplete because the complexity of 'face' is unfathomable to those not born and raised with the concept. In the next chapter we will try our best — and that's an aspect of 'face' — to explain some of the complexity.

## CHINA BUSINESS BITES

China business needs China champions. Listen to your PRC staff for insights into culture, operations and problem solving. They may be your greatest in-house asset for any China champions.

# Chapter 3

# FACE OFF

Face is your standing and reputation in the community, amongst friends and with strangers. It is all pervasive and a constant concern. Face, or *mian zi* 面子, is an integral part of your position in the community, the way you interact with society and the way society interacts with you.

Face is about respect and *yi cheng dai ren* 以诚待人 — sincerity. Face without sincerity is a falsehood and this falseness is quickly unmasked by people who have spent a lifetime assessing character as a foundation of survival. Chinese friends talk of people having a good heart. This is not a cliché. It is an assessment of sincerity.

Face is inescapable in China. Like a Sichuan quick-change opera mask performance, in China face has multiple aspects and it is found all day, every day, in every situation from private and personal, to public and professional. Face is so blindly obvious to the Chinese because it is intuitive and this makes it difficult to explain. Without even a basic understanding of face, Western businessmen are truly stumbling blindly in a minefield.

Face can be gained, or lost, given to you, or you can give to others. Face can be borrowed, or loaned. Face can be many things, but it can never be ignored and it can never be purchased.

Working in China, we must remember face for our Chinese colleagues and also face for ourselves. The two aspects are often inseparable. Something said in good-natured jest, particularly in front of others, may be taken as a loss of face. This is a problem for Westerners who typically joke in this way with friends and colleagues. This simple jesting has more serious implications with Chinese friends.

Consider the situation of a formal banquet given by a Western host, if only the Chinese guests are given chopsticks, this is a loss of face. It gives the impression the hosts think they cannot use a knife and fork. It is also a loss of face if they are given knife and fork and not chopsticks because not all are comfortable with using cutlery in a skilled way. The face saving and face giving solution is to put chopsticks together with knife and fork at every table setting

If I speak Chinese poorly but proudly identify my teacher then I cause a loss of face for her. The implication is that if she had done a better job of teaching me, my speaking ability would be better. My teacher thus loses face because my poor performance is a reflection of her teaching ability. The solution is to explain that my Chinese is poor because I am a poor student. This allows my teacher to save face. If I want my teacher to gain face then I would say I am fortunate to be taught by her, otherwise my Chinese would be even worse!

Trivial issues and responses? For Westerners, these are trivial and the responses smack of an unnecessary and contrived politeness. For the Chinese, however, these are all important considerations of face. Some are significant, some are less important and some are just an irritation, but they all reflect on face. In combination these may become a significant impediment to the way you do business or the quality of the business you undertake. Face has many aspects.

Face is public and private.

Face can be given and taken.

Face can be borrowed or lent.

Face can be lost or gained.

Face can be received or taken way.

Face is transferred by association and introduction.

Face is tangible and intangible.

In this business bite we examine just a few of these, along with some examples to give you a flavour of what is involved. This is a starting point and not an exhaustive list. It is a mistake to think of these as showing superficiality because the surface situation masks a greater depth of sincerity and respect. The examples are designed to help you think about how face is perceived so you are more aware of the situations where face is involved.

Face is not just for public use. This is where we most often see the concept in operation because public face is related to how we are perceived in the community amongst our friends, our peers and strangers. Face is also private, allowing very good friends to talk to each other in quite direct and at times apparently insulting ways without losing face. In a paradoxical fashion, this directness gives you face because it affirms the closeness of the friendship. Personal face comes from the way you treat your family, deferring to age or looking to their welfare.

Face is given when you acknowledge a person's position and status in a public environment. This may be achieved through seating arrangements, by the order in which you enter a room and by the information included on a name card. For government officials, a name card with a long list of official positions and titles gives face. It comes from the hotel you stay in, the way you eat and the way you treat others. This aspect of face involves issues of status and deference that are more easily understood in Western terms, although the associated behaviours may be different.

Face is taken away when the deference to status and position is not observed. When only your seating does not have a place card but others do. When others are introduced by position and name but you are introduced by name only and your name appears on the program with an incorrect position attributed.

Face is borrowed to increase your own face or standing. When you arrive at a meeting by taxi, and leave in the Chairman's car with his driver. When your hotel does not have enough face, you ask to be dropped off at a prestigious Western hotel. You borrow the hotel's face. You stand in the lobby waving goodbye to the driver before catching a taxi to your less prestigious hotel. You know the driver will report back to the Chairman.

Face is lent when you give your car and driver to a friend so he can play host to his friends. Face is lent when you allow others to use aspects of your position to boost their standing in public. Face is lent when you praise your colleague by acknowledging the role their work has played in your success. In the West, this acknowledgement is about teamwork and is not usually seen as an aspect of face.

Face is lost when you are not treated or acknowledged in a way appropriate to your status or position. You stay in a four-star hotel to save costs but you want to negotiate a multi-million-dollar deal. You may think this shows you want to keep business costs down but you lose face because it is interpreted as you being stingy.

You provide an inappropriate standard of accommodation for the chairman of a visiting investment delegation. This type of face is more familiar to Westerners, but not just in formal situations. This also applies in informal and relaxed situations. The host loses face at a relaxed informal dinner if you call for an extra bottle of wine because it suggests he is not attuned to your needs. Face is also lost for the host when you offer to pay for the meal because it implies you think he does not have the necessary financial resources to do so.

Face is gained, not when you are treated as you expect, but when you are treated better than you expect. This is more than being given face because the stepping up in the relationship is a permanent acknowledgement of a change in status. This extra level of treatment allows you to gain and keep face. This may be an unexpected pickup from the airport by the Chairman's car and driver. The keynote speaker acknowledges your work as part of his presentation. Your conference seating position is adjusted, or you are directed to sit next to the host. Face is gained not by what you do, but by the acknowledgement of what you have done. This is more than praise. It is an acknowledgement of a change in your status.

Face is received and acknowledged when you are treated and act in a way consistent with your standing in the group. As a foreigner at a conference it is appropriate that I speak English. I receive face because this is what is expected of me as a foreign expert. I give face to the organisers because I fill the role and expectations of a foreign expert.

Face is taken away when I speak entirely in Chinese at a conference. It takes away my standing as a foreign expert. I don't lose face because the content of my delivery is high quality but I diminish my 'foreignness' by speaking in Chinese and some of my face is taken away. I also take face away from the organiser because I am less foreign. I gain face with an introductory greeting in Chinese because this shows friendliness but I add to this face by switching back to English for the remainder of the speech.

Face is transferred by association and introduction. One of the difficulties in putting together a conference in China is that people are reluctant to accept speaking invitations until they know who else is speaking. They wish to gain face by being associated with more important people. They wish to avoid losing face by being associated with less important people. When I speak at a conference, I transfer face to other speakers of lesser importance. I gain face when I speak alongside other international speakers. The solution is to issue speaking invitations that include information on other speakers who have been invited. People are able to assess if the event will give them face or transfer face.

Introductions are not undertaken lightly. They are not a casual process because they involve multiple levels of face. Introductions form an important part of business and a way to grow business. This introduction transfer of face is also part of *guanxi* 关系 — relationship. Networks are essential to business but the networks of introduction are most successful in China. When I introduce you to a third party then my face is involved. If you fail to deliver, fail to perform or fail to live up to expectations then it is my face on the line. In accepting my introduction, the third party expects the person I have introduced will be of a certain quality. It is about trust and this lies at the foundation of relationships.

If I am the one being introduced then I need to be aware that my behaviour, my performance and my subsequent business do not just reflect on me. All of these aspects reflect on the face of the person who has introduced me. Additionally, the performance, behaviour and quality of the person I am being introduced to reflects on the face of the person who has done the introduction.

Facilitating introductions involves face for all the participants because it is an essential part of the *guanxi* 'banking' system designed to expand and develop essential networks.

Face is tangible and this is most easily understood in terms of gifts, discussed in more detail in Chapter 9. For the mid-autumn festival, I gave moon cakes to my friend Nannan who is working in Singapore. The more attractively boxed, and to some extent, the more reasonably expensive, the more tangible the face given with the gift. This concept is not too far removed from common Western thinking about gifts.

Intangible face can also be created with the same gift. Rather than buying the moon cakes for Nannan in Singapore, I purchased them for her in Beijing. This shows I made much more effort to remember and find the gift despite my busy schedule. This gives the gift the intangible aspect of face.

Face is not a single unchanging concept equally applied. It not like a licence to drive that has a recognised standard and validity in all situations. Face is variable and situational. You have different types of face in different types of situations. Face changes as your environment changes. Chinese face is more pervasive than the casualness of the Singaporeans and it has a fluidity and complexity beyond the rigid formality of the Japanese.

We can spend too much time worrying about the details of face. It is not appropriate for Westerners as we are not expected to understand the details and intricacies of face. We are given a great deal of latitude for errors and ignorance. However, face cannot be ignored. An unexpected prickly reaction you get to what was a flippant or throwaway comment tells you that you have made a face mistake. It is best to avoid this by becoming more aware of the importance your friends, colleagues and business associates attach to face. Always look at the other perspective of what you do to decide its impact on face.

*Guanxi* 关系 or relationships are based on the intricate structure of face. *Guanxi* is a currency and a banking system. Survival in China without this banking system is very difficult. In a complex, crowded society it is those who can navigate the shifting shoals of regulation who prosper. *Guanxi* at one level is about relationship power and Westerners are quickly and erroneously side tracked into Lord Acton's dictums about power and corruption. However, *guanxi* is not about corruption and those who equate *guanxi* with corruption just reveal their ignorance of the concept and its complexity.

Western taxation law and regulation is an everchanging landscape. We navigate it by employing lawyers, accountants, advisors and advisory services. We generally buy these skills although the level of service we get may vary depending upon our relationship with the principals of the firm. The larger customer gets more service than the small customer.

In China *guanxi* relationships will help you to identify the best service provider and the most appropriate person to speak to. Rather than pay for it via the anonymity of an unknown third-party service provider, many Chinese will spend guanxi capital to access the same information.

My elderly mother lives in a city far away and experienced a rapid deterioration in health. She was admitted to hospital, but was treated badly, shuffled from one bureaucratic pillar to another. Despite her having the highest levels of private health insurance I felt helpless to understand the situation and improve the outcome. My sister is a nurse in another city, so she talked to the hospital staff. She talked to the nurses and the doctors in a way that I cannot. She speaks their language, understands their processes and was able to facilitate better and more appropriate treatment for our mother simply because she knew what she was talking about. Instead of the usual six weeks the problem of care was resolved within three weeks.

In any mindless complex bureaucracy, there are advantages in what you know and who you know. My sister was able to achieve things I could not because I am outside the hospital system. No favours were done, no special services were provided, no future obligations entered into but my sister's better understanding of the system and processes meant the right questions were asked and the right answers were recognised when they were given. This is family *guanxi* in operation. Read the above again and replace 'my sister' with 'my friend' and you have a better idea of how Chinese *guanxi* operates.

*Guanxi* is not mysterious and unique to China. It is a concept familiar to the alumni of business schools and MBAs but it operates at deeper and more complex levels in China.

The Chinese open their *guanxi* accounts from the day they are born. In part it is gifted to them by their parents but they must add to this account through their own actions. Westerners do not have this advantage. As a Westerner, you open a guanxi account by making a deposit. This may come through helping someone with kindness and offering support in a time of need. It comes from being a good person, a moral person, a caring person. It comes from offering assistance before it is requested. We might call this a reserve of goodwill. You have a *guanxi* account with every significant individual you meet or with whom you want to do business.

Deposits may be made into your *guanxi* account or someone may open an account for you. The chairman of another company may ask you to take on his son as an intern and so he makes a deposit or opens a *guanxi* account with you. These are the Chinese requests for favours we are familiar with, but often we are less familiar with the long-term purpose of these. They are not favours given and forgotten, but deposits into a *guanxi* account that you can draw upon in the future. Just as with any bank account, the funds can be used for honest and ethical purposes, or for corrupt purposes. The use you put the account to is your decision.

Deposits are large and small, accumulated from small favours and considerate actions and amassed from significant deposits. I arranged for white flowers for the funeral of a friend's father who was buried in his home village. It gave unexpected face to my friend and unintentionally became a large deposit in my *guanxi* account. These accounts accumulate a growing balance and your Chinese friends keep an accurate accounting. This is not a malicious or mercenary practice. It is done as intuitively and as automatically as Western drinking friends keep track of whose turn it is to buy the next round of drinks no matter how drunk they get.

Not all relationships are created equal and the strength of obligation bonds varies, like ripples expanding from a stone thrown into a pool. The closest and most powerful bonds are between family members. Next strongest are the bonds created by shared high school and particularly shared university experiences. Beyond this are relationships created at work and with colleagues. Not quite at the furthest reaches of these relationship ripples are those with Western businesses. Over time as relationships deepen and mature you may move more towards the inner circles but you will rarely gain access to the very innermost.

Westerners do not have many *guanxi* coins to start with. It takes time to build a bank account. Many Westerners complain that the first few years in China are a constant situation of constant giving and getting little in return. This giving is the foundation of building the *guanxi* bank account. Others have a lifetime of savings, but you are starting out afresh so it takes time to save.

*Guanxi* purchased with dollars is as counterfeit as a Shenzhen DVD of the latest Hollywood movie. It will not stand the tests of time, financial stress or bankruptcy. It reflects a shallow and simplistic Western understanding of a complex system based on respect, obligation and responsibility.

Face and *guanxi* are aspects of the same universal coinage used in China. It is a foreign currency and if we want to operate in China, we must learn how to use it.

## CHINA BUSINESS BITE

Face is the foundation of everything in China. It is inescapable. *Guanxi* is an informal banking system intimately tied to face. Without face and *guanxi* there is no civilised society.

# Chapter 4

# BUSINESS THE CHINA WAY

Face is the foundation of Chinese social relationships and, not surprisingly, it is the foundation of genuine long-term business in China. You can of course just buy your business in China with a simple exchange of money and contracts. It is a meaningless transaction in a shallow relationship and predictably, it is often the source of perceived cheating, evasion and questionable practice from both the Chinese and Western sides. Long-term business is not built on such shallow foundations, particularly in a country where the rule of law is replaced by the rule of regulation.

Developing a better understanding of face is essential for understanding how to do business the China way. This is not a challenge restricted to Europeans. People of Chinese descent living outside of China in Singapore, Malaysia and elsewhere face the same challenges.

The comfortable assumption of non-PRC Chinese that "we are all Chinese so therefore we can work easily in China" is flawed. This was a painful lesson learned by the Singapore Government in its initial co-operation project — the China-Singapore Suzhou Industrial Park. It's a lesson repeatedly learned by boards of Singaporean companies as they make forays into China. As a Westerner working in China, I have developed perspectives on co-operation that resonate with Singaporean companies who are struggling to understand why their Chinese heritage gives them limited advantage in China. In some cases, it even confers significant disadvantage because Chinese expectations of Chinese-speaking foreigners are higher than their expectations of Westerners.

The Indian edition of FORBES carried an article titled "Humility, Strength, Guanxi". It was written by Laurie Underwood who with CEIBS professor Juan Antonio Fernandez, co-authored *China CEO* and *China Entrepreneur*.

Underwood suggests "there is no magic shortcut that can channel China expertise to a foreign manager; each individual must pass through an often-painful learning process."

Learning is the most difficult key. Most times when businesses go to China they are building on success in their home market. They are masters of their own universe and it is an abrupt shock to find the Chinese universe is so radically different. My field is technical analysis of financial markets and before working in China I had a well-established national and international reputation and business model. Having worked in Asia, and mainly with Chinese in Asia, I felt confident the same business model would transfer largely intact into China.

I was wrong.

Recognising this was not as simple as the three words above convey. A great deal of ego, intransience, arrogance and ignorance can be tied up in a situation like this and they all act as expensive barriers. Typically, people and organisations have a range of reaction options.

One reaction is to ignore the new universe and try to impose as much as possible of your known universe. This simply will not work and in later chapters we look at some of the consequences of this non-adaptive approach. It is often more generous, less costly and less frustrating to just take the money and donate it to the Chinese Government. When corporate giants like Rupert Murdoch and Google fail in part because they tried to impose as much as possible of their known universe on China, then the chances of success for smaller companies using similar approaches are very slim.

Another reaction is to simply walk away and put China in the too hard basket. For many this is the cheapest and the most sensible option. China business is difficult, and unless you have China champions and a willingness to expend considerable time and effort, then China business becomes virtually impossible.

The third reaction is the most difficult because it requires humility and this is a characteristic not often associated with the very business success that leads to the knocking on China's door. It is the first of many contradictions you will discover in China. The Chinese Daoist classic, the *Dao de Jing* 道德经 (Tao Te Ching) is famous in the West for its apparent tautologies. We are often told to listen to what is not said in Chinese responses. This happens when we make a suggestion and the response is lukewarm when we were expecting strong support. What is not said — strong agreement — is the most important aspect of the response. This concept of the usefulness of what is, and what is not, is an apparent contradiction and a good summary of the difficulties of working in China.

The Dao de Jing famously observes that "We turn clay to make a vessel; but it is on the space where there is nothing that the usefulness of the vessel depends. Therefore, just as we take advantage of what is, we should recognise the usefulness of what is not." Much of working in China has the same tautological duality — humility leads to its opposite, recognition and success. As Underwood writes:

> While being humble is not a characteristic added to the resumes of most top executives elsewhere in the world, it is critical for newcomers to China. A humble mind-set allows you to admit to your novice status as a China hand and thus take the steps necessary to make up for your knowledge gaps.

This is perhaps the most important thing I quickly and fortunately learned in China. I am still a China novice but I am now quicker at understanding the reasons for taking particular actions. I am a 'foreign expert' in financial markets and market trading, but my lack of Chinese language ability meant when I first went to China, I was reduced to the status of a dependent and somewhat retarded child. My inability to communicate was a humbling experience, particularly as a substantial part of my business is based on public speaking at conferences and workshops.

There are two ways to respond to this uncomfortable humbling experience. You can swim to the shallow end and this means consorting with European expats, working in offices where English is regularly spoken and eating San Francisco-style Chinese meals in Beijing where the diners are mainly Western with a sprinkling of expat Chinese and curious locals.

Or you can swim to the deep end, accepting as much assistance as possible in the spirit in which it is given. If you show a willingness to swim, you will quickly find friends who will not allow you to sink. The concept of 'good heart' *hao xin* 好心 plays an important part in developing new Chinese relationships that will guide you in business. This may sound a little new age, but in later chapters I will show you the hard edges on these apparently fuzzy concepts.

You can say "I know what I am doing in business and this is the way I have been successful in the West, so this will be successful in China." However, my choice was to accept my junior status in terms of knowledge outside my Western home market and financial market experience and start an accelerated education course from almost ground zero. I wanted to work in China so I needed to know more. If you want to work in China then you also need to know more. There is no single path to acquire this knowledge. In this book I show you the path I took.

I learn from reading so when I returned to Australia after my first working trip to Shanghai and Dalian, I commenced reading what became a hundred and fifty or more books on China. This was an eclectic mix from history, politics, culture, to modern bitterness literature drawn from the Cultural revolution experience and old and ancient Chinese novels. My Chinese friends recommended books I would never have considered or discovered by myself. These moved beyond the thematic of *Wild Swans* and political tocsins of *Red Dust* so appealing to Western audiences. It included rugged unsentimental memoirs along the lines of *Half Man Is Woman* and *Fortress Besieged.*

My reading included Western perspectives of Chinese culture, from the unsympathetic Lord Macartney *An Embassy to China* to the more perceptive *Chinese Etiquette and Business Ethics* by Boye Lafayette De Mente and the modern experience in *River Town* by Peter Hessler. Where possible, I read translations of Chinese history written by Chinese scholars. I included modern fiction set in China because this genre gives Qiu Xiaolong in *When Red Is Black* and Nicole Mones in

*Lost in Translation* more freedom to explore the characteristics of behaviour.

History shapes the future and our understanding of history distorts our understanding of the present. I went to school during the Vietnam War — the American War from the Chinese perspective — and there was an unprecedented curriculum focus on Asian history. Not surprisingly it was history written from a British and American perspective with clear heroes and villains. No prizes for guessing who was which.

The Chinese understanding of their history is of course different, but not in the way you might expect. There are jingoistic elements just as there are in Western history. However, Chinese understanding of their history is more deeply entrenched, more profound, and more relevant to everyday life than is common in the West. History is not a dead hand of the past. Chinese history is a living force that delivers a vision of the future. Films based on Western historical events the equivalent of the *Battle of Redcliff* do not enjoy the same ready acceptance this genre has in China.

Having some familiarity with a different conception of Chinese history is an advantage because this is part of the Chinese concept of a civilised person. *A History of Chinese Civilisation* by French historian Jacques Gernet (translated by J Foster and C Hartman) is an excellent introduction to shift one's perspective because he is not steeped in the British imperial tradition of history. His account is not overtly anti-Western, nor overtly pro-Chinese.

Look at this history from different perspectives and you encounter something disturbing. Julia Lovell in *The Opium Wars* reveals this in her discussion of the way adverse images of the Chinese were deliberately created as part of a political campaign in the British press to lay the foundations for justifying the Opium Wars. That's a trick as old as politics itself, but the truly disturbing aspect is the way these images, these phrases of abuse, these stereotypes of celestial avarice, corruption and moral turpitude are repeated almost word for word in today's Hollywood films, newspaper columns, letters to the editor, by political speech writers and several global leaders.

Not everyone is a reader, and my solutions are not a panacea. You do not have to follow this path but a similar level of commitment is required. My personal solutions are an example of the type of effort required to build solid foundations for lasting business. Expansion into China is not an incremental step for your existing business. It is almost the equivalent of starting a new business.

You can have a business with China with less effort, but it will always teeter on the edge of disaster. Minor setbacks become crises and then the business fails. Solid foundations allow businesses to survive major setbacks and emerge stronger and more effective. These include external economic shocks like the GFC and COVID-19. That's my objective, and as a reader of this book, I assume it is also your objective. It's the difference between being too hard to pursue, and too interesting to ignore.

Too much reading? Then try talking. I found learning the basics of language offered insights into thinking well beyond the benefits of mere translation. Basic Chinese may be disparagingly described as Starbucks Chinese, meaning you know enough to get around, order a meal, and do some basic shopping. But even Starbucks Chinese provides insights you would never have if you remain monolingual. The challenges and benefits of learning Chinese, or some Chinese, are discussed in later chapters.

My Chinese colleagues, many of whom later became my friends recognised this rapid decision that I needed to learn to work the China way. They became my mentors in this education process. My China education continues as long as I am prepared to learn.

I'm not suggesting my solution is the ideal, or only solution. Everybody takes a different road, but the common path starts with humility — itself more of a Chinese concept than a Western one where it is too often confused with submissiveness. Understanding that you do not know is the first step to developing knowledge.

Failure is always an option in China but the roots of failure often lie within ourselves because we are poor or unwilling students. When failure comes it is all too easy to place the blame where it does not belong and using a foreign scapegoat is so tempting. In the next chapter, we start with the negatives of business failure, and then use these to extract some of the core business bites for success.

## CHINA BUSINESS BITES

China business inevitably requires some reassessment of historical perspectives. It may also require some adjustments to the way you do business. China need not be a humbling experience but humility is a path to success.

# Chapter 5

# ESSENCE OF FAILURE

Silver chopsticks are used in Korea because, according to tradition, the silver will turn black if the food is poisoned. These summary notes are simple tarnished silver chopsticks showing the presence of business poison. The reasons for business failure are more complex than these small bites suggest but they provide the flavour of failure and its ingredients. Recognise how to avoid these and it becomes easier to appreciate the flavours of success.

When foreign companies fail in China, they often blame the Chinese Government's policy and restrictions. Some companies avoid working in China because they believe these reports. The Chinese regulatory environment is confusing, but this is not an excuse for failure. Often, failure comes from a more basic level because companies fail to understand the competitive environment. Part of the China syndrome is the belief that the Chinese will love your service simply because it is foreign and it is yours, or that there is no effective competition to your service existing in China so it is a largely regulation-free environment.

Does this sound a little harsh? Google and eBay were headline business failures in China and they laid the blame squarely on unfair and restrictive competitive practices. It's a narrative easily accepted by some US business and political leaders. Whilst the reasons for failure are complex, there are some basic factors which have contributed and they cannot be ignored.

Baidu, Google's Chinese competitor, succeeded because it offered services Google would not offer. Google made much of censorship issues but these complaints appealed more to Western perceptions and to a comparatively small population of Chinese dissidents than it did to the bulk of potential users in China. Chinese users felt more comfortable with a service constructed in their local language (rather than a poor Chinese translation) that was fully linked up with Chinese web sites. Google failed to offer services its users wanted.

eBay misread the Chinese market situation on several levels, perhaps believing it was large and powerful enough to force its requirements upon the potential user base. eBay charged for site listings while its Chinese competitors did not. eBay put its services on servers outside of China, and as a result slowed the transaction time considerably. In a competitive bidding environment, time lags become significant. eBay did not offer a way for buyers and sellers to chat online, but their competitors did. Chinese buyers like to talk with sellers, to haggle about quality and price. eBay's Chinese competitors understood this and included it as a value-add service.

These factors reveal a basic underestimation of the competition landscape but many supporters of these US companies believed their Chinese competitors had an unfair advantage because they "often maintain close ties with regulators which helps them to anticipate new policies".

In the US this is called lobbying and Google spent more than 21 million on this in 2019. During the depths of the global financial crisis in 2008, General Motors and Ford were successful in obtaining US Government-backed bailouts whilst the Japanese car maker Toyota battled a hostile environment of public opinion over allegations of sticky accelerators. The different treatments reflected a difference in the ability to maintain close ties with regulators.

Problems with lobbying are not often used as an excuse for business failure. Toyota did not pull out of the US. Instead it complied with changes in regulations and adjusted its business model.

American web giants failed in China because they failed to listen to customers. They did not fail mainly because of the malevolent activity of the Chinese Government. Chinese companies face the same maze of bureaucracy, the same political constraints, the same changing regulations as foreign companies. They overcome these obstacles by working within the system rather than appealing to the way a 'superior' foreign regulatory system works. Unlike foreign managers, they do not complain China is not like home because China is home.

The reality of international business is that foreign business cannot change the regulations and laws of the country in which they are operating. Foreign customers have different needs and habits and successful selling takes these into account. It is part of market research rather than a blind belief that your product or service is so good that everybody will want it. Learning how to do business in a foreign country is an unavoidable challenge because, to use the American saying, "you are not in Kansas anymore".

These experiences of failure are important. China is arguably the largest economy in the world. China is now second only to the US as a destination for foreign direct investment. These are not insignificant achievements for an economy routinely described as closed, too restricted or too difficult to work in.

Corporate arrogance is inexcusable but understandable in the sense that despite the best efforts of local managers, it is ultimately up to the head offices to make the smart decisions. You would expect that smaller companies, or individuals would be more aware of these problems and be able to act more quickly to resolve them. It is not always the case.

## CHINA BUSINESS BITES

Failure is easy in China when companies fail to do appropriate market research. Take a realistic look at competitors and the reasons for their success. Blaming the Chinese Government and regulations for business failure is a coward's excuse.

# Chapter 6

# SENSE AND SENSIBILITY

In Western business we are protected by the company and the organisation. Individuals may fail but generally the company continues as a separate entity. China is a lot more personal. What you say, and how you say it may have a larger impact than you expect. Sense and sensibility play a much larger role than the straight-talking crash through or crash approach. It is no accident that Jane Austen's books are popular reading for students learning English. Their focus on manners touches a common chord.

How you pitch is in many ways more important than what you pitch. We look at some failures and some solutions. At a Chinese financial conference in Shenzhen, I listened to a renowned and successful American financial trader give a presentation to a Chinese audience. Forget for the moment the subject matter. It could just as well be your presentation about a business proposal or an explanation of an area of your professional expertise to a meeting in China, or to a Chinese delegation in your home city.

One of the interesting aspects of this presentation was the way the speaker completely misunderstood the thinking and aspirations of his audience. Listening to the comments from the few Europeans in the audience, it was clear they found his presentation inspiring, insightful and useful in a practical way.

Listening to the comments from the Chinese in the audience however, I realised they found his presentation irrelevant, and almost useless; yet they had come to hear the same information as the few

Westerners in the audience. They had wanted to learn about the practical application of these trading methods to financial markets.

The first task of a speaker is to create empathy and relevance. The American speaker did this by showing a few slides highlighting the lifestyle results that making money in the market can deliver. It was a Western dream. After achieving success, he moved from the city to the countryside, living in a rustic farmhouse with a barn, upgraded with modern broadband internet access. He raised animals, played in fields of corn and owned a collection of vintage tractors. He sported a suntan which showed he worked outside the confines of an office.

Every European in the room was swooning at this return to an idyllic rural paradise. The speaker had shown the lifestyle benefits of a successful business in the financial markets. It was an ambition they could identify with.

The Chinese audience was appalled. Their ambition is to leave the countryside, to get away from peasant roots as quickly possible. The prospect of developing a suntan would mark them clearly as *nong min* 农民 — farmer or peasant. This is the very antithesis of success in modern China. The audience aspires to a modern apartment in the Chinese equivalent of a gated community where the manual work is done by *xiao shi gong ren* 小时工人 — workers paid by the hour to do menial work like gardening.

The speaker lost many of his audience in the first five minutes of his 90-minute presentation. When he moved on to explaining some of the core of his trading methods, he regained some of the audience, but he quickly lost them again with well-rehearsed American humour. He had repeated this particular presentation many times in the US and Europe, so he clearly knew when to pause for laugher. He prided himself on his bluntness and told his audience how he always told the truth when people asked him for his opinion of their trading skills. "That's why I have no friends," he joked. The Westerners in the audience chuckled while his Chinese audience sat in stony silence, quickly deciding mentally that skill without face or friends is not a desirable outcome.

A person without friends is a poor man in Chinese terms. He has no *guanxi* 关系 — relationship power — and cannot help his friends or be helped by others. He is isolated. The Chinese audience pride themselves on their ability to avoid conflict. Bluntness is not polite and demonstrates bad manners.

The speaker's lack of understanding of the aspirations of his audience, his failure to understand behaviours valued by his audience and his belief that his brand of humour was universally funny meant the real value of his experience and his ability to trade in financial markets was lost to his audience.

Of course, he blamed the quality of his translator for the lacklustre response from his audience. His translator had modified some of the more offensive speaker comments, had taken the time to explain in more detail some of the points not properly explained by the speaker, and had done his best to explain the American jokes. You try translating "Your trading just goes to hell in a hand cart" and also capture the meaning at the same time. "Your trading will have big problems" was a good translation.

The failure here was not just a failure to understand his audience. It was failure to connect with the audience because of an assumption that the audience shared the same values as the speaker. Although the audience and the speaker desired the same outcome — the benefits of successful market trading — their conception of those benefits were very different.

This confusion is a major obstacle in other areas, including marketing. The pursuit of feminine beauty is universal, but it took some time for Western cosmetic companies to understand Chinese women did not aspire to makeup that produced tanned skin that is so desirable to many Western women. Chinese women aspired to white skin because it showed they did not have to work in the sun. Success came to Western cosmetic companies when they understood skin lightening cosmetics were the desired beauty solution. They could of course have taken a leaf from the Japanese cosmetic companies which had already exploited these differences.

This confusion is a major obstacle in political relations. Some in the United States have recently discovered that thriving capitalism in China did not, as they expected, lead to a liberal democracy. They failed to understand their audience.

Working with a delegation of investors from China may appear to revolve around a single clear objective, but the reasons for attaining that objective may be different from the ones you imagine. The most challenging aspect of China business is the constant need to reassess your assumptions. The surface appearances may appear similar, but the structure beneath the surface is very different. Failure to examine those assumptions underpins many business failures at a corporate and personal level.

Talking to mainland Chinese audiences is a tough job, whether it be in Shanghai, or to a visiting delegation in London or Sydney. With a little forethought you can talk the language of your Chinese audience without knowing how to speak Chinese. The result is better business and easier and more accurate translation.

Enough of the negatives. Business can and does succeed in China but the seeds of success grow in a foreign soil and sprout in unexpected places. In the remaining chapters of this section we concentrate on what some may consider to be small things, but they assume a greater degree of significance in the Chinese environment.

## CHINA BUSINESS BITES

Translation is not the problem. It is what has to be translated that may be the problem. You lose in translation when your starting assumptions are foreign. Talk the language of your audience, or business partners and the translation will be smoother and more accurate.

# Chapter 7

# INVEST IN CHINA BUSINESS

Mount Tai Shan is one of the five sacred mountains in China. It's a 1,545-metre behemoth rising abruptly from the Shandong plain with thousands of steps cut into its steep sides. It has been climbed by numerous emperors and untold millions of tourists. Getting to the top is an arduous process.

You cannot run to the top of Tai Shan. It is not sustainable. If you want to get to the top you have to take a steady pace to avoid exhaustion.

Transferring the simple mathematics of capital accumulation to market growth seems difficult. The rule of 72 in investing tells us a 6% return will double our capital in twelve years. A growth rate of 6% in an economy will have the same effect but it's much more difficult to do for an entire economy than it is for a single private investment account.

China continues to aim for 6% growth, down from 7% or more in previous years. This does not represent a collapse, or massive slowdown, of the Chinese economy. Even at this lower rate it suggests a doubling in size in a little more than ten years. Reality suggests this is a difficult target to achieve.

It's all in the numbers and it's a function of size. When you are small it is easy to double your growth. As you get larger, doubling becomes more difficult by several orders of magnitude. According to myth, the Indian advisor who asked for only 1 grain of rice on the first square of the chessboard, and two grains on the next square until all 64 squares had been bought into the calculation soon consumed more than the total Indian rice production.

The reality is that once a critical mass is achieved, growth begins to slow. It doesn't mean opportunity diminishes. More than half a century of growth at 2% to 3% in the US did not prevent it from becoming the birthplace of Microsoft, Google, Dow chemicals and other industry giants. A slowing of growth in China from the unsustainable 8% or more to a more sustainable lower level will change the nature of opportunity but not diminish the opportunity. The challenge for investors is to identify the changes in the paradigm and invest accordingly.

Climbing Tai Shan includes very steep sections. It includes some dips and gentle inclines all within the context of unrelenting upwards pressure to reach the top. When markets are startled by lower or higher PMI (Purchasing Managers' Index) figures, by the gyrations of quarterly growth figures and the ebb and flow of monetary easing, it is useful to remember how we can get to the top of Tai Shan by taking the longer view of the journey. We should not let a leaf block our view of Tai Shan.

If we believe in China's growth, then how can we access it via the market when the mainland stock market is largely closed to foreign investment? There are several ways to invest in mainland China markets. Investors who are nervous about direct investment in Chinese markets, or investment in Chinese companies listed on the Western stock exchanges have several alternatives. This is investment in companies doing business in China or with China. The distinction is important.

There are five methods available to invest in Chinese economic growth.

The first is by using an Exchange Traded Fund (ETF) that tracks the Shanghai Index. As expected, this ETF gives investors a return matching the performance of the underlying index. However not all China 'index' funds are the same. Some include a mixture of mainland and Hong Kong listed Red Chips. These ETFs provide another method to participate in the China market. My preference is for direct exposure to the Shanghai Index.

The second method is direct investing in mainland companies. This is enabled by the Cross Connect program and participating brokers.

I do not read Chinese quickly enough to apply fundamental analysis, so stock selection is based on pure technical and chart analysis. The focus is on strong trend behaviour and trend breakouts. This is the same methods technical traders apply to Western markets.

Direct investing is not for everyone so there are three alternatives which offer a proxy for investing in the Chinese economy. The advantage of these approaches is that investors may be more familiar with these locally listed companies and have more confidence in their management and reporting procedures.

These methods carry individual company risk so a bad choice can underperform the Shanghai Index and a good choice can outperform.

The first group of stocks are companies that export to China and which have a direct relationship with the strength of the economy. Companies doing business *with* China are those who rely on China as a customer. Think the Australian resource companies BHP, Rio, Fortesque Metals and a host of smaller companies sending raw materials to China. Consumer consumption stocks like Australia's A2 milk have well-developed consumer acceptance in China.

Investing in China growth at arm's length by investing in companies that do business with China is an effective solution. It removes the risk associated with trying to grow a business in China. Extracting resources from the ground does not involve mastering new business paradigms so the risk of business failure is lower. Of course, individual company risk remains.

The second group is companies that have a well-established domestic business in China. These are companies doing business *in* China. Like Starbucks they may be part of an international chain, but the business is still very local in China. Singapore group, Food Republic provides this investment avenue with stores in Beijing and elsewhere. Another Singapore group, CapitaLand has a number of shopping malls in tier 1 and tier 2 cities.

KFC, Starbucks, Macdonald's, Wal-Mart and dozens of others that have established business dominance in their home country. GM sells more cars in China than its combined total sales in the rest of the world. They have come to realise China is not an undeveloped country and that competition is fierce and well-developed. Investing in these companies as a means of tapping into the growth of China carries a range of risks.

There is the usual risk of company mismanagement, failure to appreciate changes in the marketplace and sustaining growth in mature markets. These are the normal metrics of investment analysis. But added to these are the dangers of getting it wrong with the development in China. For many years KFC was far more successful in its China expansion than MacDonald's because it adapted its menu and marketing to meet Chinese preferences. Whilst KFC, with its tiered branding, may be a second choice as an investment in this industry segment in the West, it was a first choice for investment for China exposure.

These companies are directedly plugged into the growth of the Chinese economy and the consumer recovery, but they are listed on Western stock exchanges.

The final approach is to select companies that are importing from China. This is now a more dangerous approach because of the push to reduce reliance on China and broaden supply lines. These are companies that rely on the recovery of Chinese manufacturing for their own growth because their business models are based on Chinese imports. In the US this includes Apple. Other companies reliant on Chinese imports include Walmart. Closer to home the Australian conglomerate Westfarmers runs the large-scale hardware chain, Bunnings. The vast majority of their product line comes from China. The risk in these investments is that the growth of the company depends not just on Australian demand but also on the ability of Chinese suppliers to quickly get back into business.

These five options provide good choices for investing in the continuing Chinese economic recovery. Despite the anti-China push by some countries there is no doubt that the Chinese economy will continue to expand, so it should be part of every investment portfolio.

A century ago, America was referred to as 'gold mountain' by the Chinese. Now the appellation is applied to China but as in every gold mine there is a lot of worthless material between the gold nuggets.

These days everything appears to be made in China, and rumour has it that Santa Claus is actually Chinese! Rumours peddled at the highest level in America also claim that US manufacturing and industry is being drowned in a sea of cheap Chinese imports and this lies at the heart of their economic woes. For some in the US, the solution is a change in the value of the yuan. For others the solution is the destruction of competition by banning Huawei, TikTok and other advanced Chinese services to give US services time to catch up.

China changes the business paradigm, making old business unprofitable and opening up opportunities for new business models. Jobs disappear in some sectors of the economy, but they reappear in other sectors. A recent US Federal Reserve Bank report concludes the total amount of all imports — goods and services — from China equals 1.9% of US consumer spending. Total US imports remained largely steady over the past 10 years, but Chinese imports replaced products from other foreign exporters.

The "Made in China" label obscures the level of foreign participation, and profit, in the product. It is estimated that on average 55% of the price paid by US consumers for goods imported from China goes to US companies and workers. These are the sales staff, the advertising agencies, the store managers and an entire domestic supply chain.

Speaking in Sydney, the then head of the World Trade Organisation, Pascal Lamy confirmed that in many cases, China was assembling imported parts and only a relatively small amount of the value was added in China. We need to be more cautious when it comes to simplistic assumptions that a "Made in China" tag means profits for China and little profit for foreign businesses.

It is certainly true that China's largest export to Western countries is deflation but the 'flood' of Chinese exports is a foundation for new ways of making a profit for Western companies and a foundation of successful business for those who are prepared to embrace new business models. Apple and Walmart are outstanding examples of this adaptation. The demise of business dinosaurs should not be confused with the end of Western business opportunities.

Your business success in China may rest on investing in businesses that have success in China or on understanding how they established success. Let someone else do the hard work. Success has many paths and you do not always need to build your own road, so we will look at some elements others have used to develop successful solutions next.

## CHINA BUSINESS BITE

China is changing business economics worldwide. You can jump on the new train, or complain. Investing in the China story is achieved by working with companies that do business in or with China but do not ignore the specific company risk.

# Chapter 8

## SUCCESS

This is Chapter eight and with eight being a lucky number for the Chinese, it is appropriate that this chapter deals with success. Shopping at my local supermarket in Beijing for the first time in several months I noticed a significant change. The chocolate section had expanded to three times its previous size. For most people that's not important, but for an unreformed chocoholic like myself this is significant. It is also significant for Western business in China because it underlines a change in the approach to the China market. It is changing from a dumping ground for unmodified Western goods and services to a market deserving of more serious consideration.

By a 'dumping ground' I refer to the practice of exporting goods to China with little or no modification to their original packaging or promotion the West. The China market is different and many companies have failed in China because they fail to recognise this difference. For years the higher-end European Lindt, Ferrero Rocher and the very low end Kinder chocolate outperformed chocolate sales in China. The US and British based companies assumed this was due to the flavour of European chocolate. They concluded the Chinese did not like chocolate.

The unusual exception was the high sales of Hershey kisses.

Anyone who has eaten a chocolate Kit Kat manufactured in Singapore will instantly know the difference from an Australian or British Kit Kat because they have a much higher sugar content. Ever keen to expand market share, the chocolate companies assumed a flavour change by reducing the sugar content would bring market share just as it had in Singapore. It did not.

This poor thinking led to all sorts of expensive and ultimately relatively useless advertising campaigns for chocolate in China. The most significant error in misunderstanding the reason for the dominance of the European brands was not so much the taste, but the packaging.

Although in China, and much to the disgust of many Americans, food at the table is shared from common serving plates, individual servings of food are not taken by hand from a common source. To offer someone a piece of chocolate from a block, or a large wrapped bar of chocolate, requires the chocolate piece to be broken off and taken by hand. In contrast, you can offer an individually wrapped Lindt, or Ferrero Rocher or Kinder chocolate with hygienic decorum. Individually wrapped chocolate serves are compatible with the Chinese sense of food hygiene.

At one level, the answer to increased market share was pretty much that simple.

Finally, the US manufacturers caught on, finally recognising and building on the accidental success of Hershey Kisses in individually wrapped sachets. Now the expanded chocolate aisles are filled with mini Kit Kats, boxes of individually wrapped Cadbury chocolates and smaller serves of Hershey chocolates alongside their individually wrapped European competitors. Competition for supermarket shelf space in China is as fierce as anywhere in the world, so the expansion of the chocolate section is significant.

This reflects an important change in thinking that needs to be applied by all businesses, large and small, seeking to penetrate the China market. The Chinese customer counts. They will not gratefully accept your product or service just because it has a foreign premium. The product or service must be good for purpose, and it must be packaged and presented in a way appropriate for the customer base.

It is marketing 101 but it is astounding how many companies fail this introductory course and go on to lose a lot of money in China. Your work in China should not duplicate these failures. It should seek to emulate the components of success.

Success for foreign companies in China is often elusive. Although it is often considered necessary to have a China strategy, many companies embark on China ventures with very little insight, great hopes, and low chances of success. Investors who want exposure to the China growth story need to be able to evaluate the potential for success for companies that are engaged with China. Companies using the wrong strategy wreak destruction on their share price and your investment in them.

There are three essential features for foreign company success in China. They apply to large corporates and to smaller enterprises. Also look for these features when investing in listed companies with business in China.

First are businesses offering status and value on products or services. It is very difficult to compete on price in China, so the field of competition must be different. It's a strategy of "luring the tiger from the mountains" 调虎离山之计 *diao hu li shan zhi ji* as the Chinese saying goes. The tiger has an advantage in the dense forests in the mountains, but he is vulnerable on the open plains. If you cannot compete on price in the jungle of the Chinese marketplace, then compete in some different area where you have a natural advantage. This includes status and service quality.

Chinese consumers are extremely value-conscious as witnessed on a small-scale daily with incessant bargaining for everything they buy. It is difficult to win on price. More importantly, Chinese consumers are very status-conscious. Many Chinese will pay very little for basic everyday items, but they are willing to pay more for goods or experiences that give face and enhance their social status, because this delivers social value beyond the price paid.

These consumer differences have become larger with the pervasive penetration of WeChat and other social media. These personalised recommendations gives face and transfer face.

Middle class consumers shop at supermarkets and department stores for everyday basics but then they go to the high-end stores like Louis Vuitton to buy high status face items. The high-end fashion and accessory chains are good investments for China exposure.

Second, and increasingly important are brands the Chinese trust. This is particularly in the food sector where food safety has become an important issue. It is an opening New Zealand has exploited with its clean food image.

Chinese have a sophisticated taste for food. Despite this, the US fast-food chains such as McDonald's, Yum! and KFC have done well in China because they are consistent in quality and perceived as offering safe food. These are characteristics Chinese companies are just beginning to develop as a competitive edge. Chains like the hot pot Haidilao and the meat-heavy XiBei restaurants have expanded because they offer the same consistent quality and safe food. They take market share from the Western brands. High-end trustworthy international brands have a premium but it is no longer as easy to establish a presence in China.

Third is foreign businesses that understand their local market — not the China market. This sounds contradictory but it's a mistake to treat China as a single consumer entity. Tastes in Shanghai are very different to tastes in Beijing or Xi'an. Many Chinese cities are the population size of small countries and viable markets just by themselves. China is a collection of different regional markets. Each has its own consumer habits and preferences. Superficially the malls may look similar, but the retail and consumer patterns are different.

Our focus on Beijing and Shanghai is understandable. These are the headline cities of China, but it is also important to remember the so-called second tier cities. In 2004, I was invited to deliver a workshop in China's north eastern port city of Dalian for the Dalian Futures Exchange. I had not heard of Dalian and I was unaware of the Exchange despite it being the second largest commodity exchange in the world as measured by turnover in Soybean futures contracts.

Second tier cities like Dalian, Nanjing, Changsha and others have populations of around 5 to 6 million. This is a significant market base within the city. Exporters to China often imagine the China market as a single entity, and then discover the complexity of distribution, advertising, regional differences and other complicating factors.

The modern variation of the Shanghai Tailors' dream suggests if only 2% of the population purchased your export product, then sales would be massive. Such thinking fails to recognise the complexity and diversity of the China market.

An alternative to taking on all of China is to develop good market penetration in a much smaller area. It's the reverse of the Shanghai Tailors' dream. It is large sales to a smaller population. A population base of 5.4 million in Dalian makes this a reasonably sized single market. Depending on the product or service you wish to export, it may well be that a single second-tier city has a sufficient customer base to make exporting a profitable venture. It is certainly easier to develop the logistics, the contacts, the distribution and advertising when it is focussed on a single city.

Businesses profit from their understanding of this regional diversity. For many years the most profitable store for Giorgio Armani in China was in the city of Taiyuan. This is a large, heavily polluted coal-mining city in northern China. Taiyuan has many very rich coal-mine bosses. Their purchasing power sustained Armani, Louis Vuitton and others. Look for companies that understand the regional advantages in China rather than those that just have a blanket China strategy.

This is a competitive market and companies that choose to play on the basis of price will fail. The advantage for foreign companies is in status branding, quality trustworthiness and diversity of regional strategies.

Although these approaches involve risk, they are the coward's approach to China because it is China at arm's length. On a personal level the challenges we face in direct engagement with China are smaller, more immediate and more profound. It's the nuts and bolts of building business in China that we turn our attention to next and it starts at the table.

## CHINA BUSINESS BITES

The Chinese customer counts. The Chinese customer has different tastes and expectations so success comes from understanding the local market within the context of the China environment.

# Chapter 9

# GREET, MEET, SEAT, TREAT AND GIVE

Greeting, introductions, meetings, and seating provide a minefield of formality that is very foreign to Western practices. To treat means to negotiate terms and the result is a treaty. It is an old-fashioned word that has fallen into disuse, but it still applies in its original meaning in China. In the classless society nothing is so important as status. Greeting, meeting, and seating are a first stumbling blocks prior to the actual process of negotiation.

It's a long process so this is a long chapter. The details matter because by avoiding confusion and embarrassment, you stand a better chance of making a good impression and a creating a smooth start to a longer relationship.

We start with name cards even though these are increasingly irrelevant. However old Western habits and thinking take a long time to die out so it remains useful to know how to use name cards in the modern Chinese environment. We deal with these antique practices first before moving onto the modern practice.

## It's in the Cards

Greeting guests starts with introductions, and business cards are used to start the process. This is rapidly fading but because it is still used in some situations, we will look at the details. Be warned, the details are not the same as usually proclaimed by many commentators.

We need to move beyond the basics of handing a business card held in both hands with the translated side up. Presenting your card incorrectly won't lose you a deal but it sends a small unfavourable message. Handing out business cards to all and sundry as is the practice in Singapore also sends an unintended message because this scatter-gun approach does not acknowledge status and face.

Is your business card the equivalent of a short novel, full of details, telephone numbers, offices, and business description? This is very much the style of business cards used in America and Europe. Increasingly this style is also appearing in much of Asia and is used to reflect the international spread of business.

The short novel remains a common style for low level businesses in China where the business card is used as a small advertisement. Participants in the Guangzhou Trade Fairs are familiar with the mini-storybook business cards delivered by printers offering fast printing services. The typeface is small, the card is crowded, and the details are excessive.

For your introduction to business in China this is the very opposite of the message you want to send. It is already difficult to compete with your potential Chinese partners in terms of size. A small Chinese company probably employs more than your entire staff, so you want to create the impression of size and stability. A business card that mimics those handed out by very small-scale Chinese companies therefore will not achieve your desired outcome.

The higher up the business order you go, the less detail is required on a business card. We see this to a limited extent in Western companies, but the phenomenon is much more prevalent in China. The CEO of a company may simply list the company name, his name, his position, and a contact number. The assumption is if you are given this card, then you will know who it is from and what his business is. No need for a short story on the card.

People with 'substantial' names — famous people — will present a card that carries only a personal name, and no contact number or email. No position is shown. Whilst we might call this an arrogance, it is a common feature of business cards for executives at the C-suite level, CEO, CIO, CFO, and above in China. Important people are not available for direct contact so the card will not carry a direct line number. A small number of people may be given a direct number, but this will be handwritten on the name card. Forget the Japanese lessons about defacing a business card by writing on it. Handwriting in China is a signal you have been given privileged access.

To some extent these changes in behaviour is about numbers. There are simply too many potential contacts and it is so easy to rapidly build up a collection of hundreds of business cards. Separating the useful from the useless and the significant from the trivial is a challenge. Significant introductions are often made by a trusted third party rather than through the accidental networking so favoured by Western conference organisers. In this more personalised situation, cards are usefully exchanged rather than collected en masse.

In Singapore, Malaysia, Vietnam; Berlin, London, New York and Sydney, a business card has become a type of advertisement and a means of making contact. Swapping emails and SMS is used as a better method of personal introduction and contact. In China, the C-level business card remains a means of personal introduction with a secondary function of a means of making contact.

This means cards are not distributed freely. Cards are often distributed quite frugally, and cards are not always given in exchange. In China if you are given one of these cards then you are expected to know this person and his high position so as a result the card may carry very little detail. You may be given a card but there is no obligation to give your card in return if you are in the senior position. You may present a card but find none is offered in return simply because your position is considered insufficient. It would seem such a rebuff when stepping off the flight from Singapore, Tokyo, or Hong Kong where cards flutter like confetti in meetings.

This is a bit of a problem for the smaller businesses that lack the instant recognition of global branding. You want to use the business card as a small advertisement. You want to be available and contactable, so there is a contradiction between the business card full of detail — which in China shows you are just a very small business — and a card with minimal detail, that shows you are a large and important business and person.

The solution is to have two sets of business cards. One is the traditional small advertisement style of card that can be given to anyone. The other is somewhere higher up the scale — your name, position, and company name. This is a face card and given to selected people only.

Give the first small novel card to a representative from the company you want to do business with. Where possibly, get staff or your translator to give this card rather than yourself. Big people, important people, company owners and managers do not undertake low level tasks like handing out business advertisement cards. Others will do this on your behalf and the fact staff do this for you confirms your status and position in a society which is purported to be classless.

Also, just because you are asked for a card does not mean you have to give one. I speak at many financial conferences and I am constantly dogged by journalists and others wanting cards. In most cases I simply apologise and say I have run out of cards. It's a transparent excuse but it saves face all round and is readily accepted. Where necessary, my staff will give a journalist a contact number but rarely a card.

The second face card is for when you met with the CEO or manager of the company you want to do business with. This card you present yourself, person to person. The usual rules apply. Present the card held in both hands. Make sure the card text is facing the receiver so it can be read easily. You will of course be using a two-sided card with one side in English and the other side in simplified — not traditional — Chinese so the Chinese side will be facing up. If you are important enough, he will remember you without the need for a busy and crowded business card advertisement.

When you accept his card, it will be done with both hands and you will take the time to read the details on the card. If you can read Chinese, then you may flip the card over to read the Chinese side. Taking the time to read is a small gesture of respect for the person who gives you the card. If the respect is not reciprocated, then you have already gained an important insight into the potential for future business and will need to adjust the conduct of the meeting accordingly.

In China in terms of business cards, less often means more.

## Stepping Above the Cards

Cards, and the etiquette that surrounds them, are almost quaint in their antiquity in modern China. They have been replaced by a QR code scan with WeChat and everybody in China has WeChat on their phone. If you do not have WeChat, then you have almost stumbled at first base because WeChat is so ubiquitous in the modern environment. Your only reasonable excuse is if you are a government official from a country where WeChat is banned from official phones.

You may be asked for a WeChat scan, or you may ask your counterpart for a WeChat scan of the QR code. It's a good idea to practice both scanning and being scanned so you can complete the task with the aplomb of an experienced user.

Scanning, or being scanned in a business situation is a step above exchanging even C-level cards. It is an open invitation to communicate on a much more personal level and carries with it a higher level of commitment than is implied with the exchange of name cards. This is also why personal WeChat QR codes are not included on name cards which may be handed out to less significant people.

In many situations, cards are simply readily accepted from less important people, and often disposed of at a later date. The really important contacts are recorded and saved by WeChat and this includes Chinese officials.

If you ask for a WeChat scan and are given a name card instead then your lower position has been politely confirmed. That's useful to know because it provides useful information when the time comes to formalise the meeting arrangements.

## Meet

Confucian concepts of hierarchy and respect were not destroyed by the Cultural Revolution and its aftermath. They went underground and remain a core part of the Chinese genetic code. The person who gets to enters an elevator first or last is not an accidental decision. It's a carefully and intuitively constructed queue. It's a queue thrown into disarray and confusion when a Westerner stands aside and invites ladies to enter first. The confusion is less in Shanghai than in Beijing, but it is still there.

Meetings are always structured and this impacts on seating. This also applies to hosting delegation, be they Chinese delegations to the West, or Western delegations in China. Better meetings start with the guest list. Confusion also starts with the guest list and impacts on seating. We need to start with constructing a better guest list, so the Chinese side understands who is and is not important without the need for complex analysis and translation.

Mixing the alphabet with Chinese characters is interesting and difficult. Add to this the increasingly common use of *Hanyu Pinyin* on computer keyboards and the limits of confusion are almost boundless. *Hanyu Pinyin* uses the Western alphabet for Chinese words.
For instance:

My English name is Daryl Guppy.

In *Hanyu Pinyin* the literal translation is *dai ruo gu bi*, in Chinese characters it is 戴若顾比.

On a formal guest list, it is 大师顾比. Notice that the first two characters have changed.

Western guest lists are simple. We put two or three important people at the top, and then the rest of the guest list is in alphabetical order. When Western delegations prepare for visits to China, they are often asked to prepare a list of participants in the delegation. The immediate Western response is to send a list showing the alphabetical order of delegation members, with one or two of the most important people listed at the top of the list. We send the delegation list to our Chinese hosts blissfully unaware of the complications this creates.

This creates a problem because the list is also used by the Chinese hosts as a guest list for banquets and functions. It is their key reference point for seating arrangements.

Western thinking suggests it is important the leaders of the delegation are recognised but it is less important for other members of the delegation to be recognised by position. This is not the case when the hosts come to arrange banquet seating, introductions, and ceremonies. Everybody has a position and a rank, and correct placement is essential.

A guest list in alphabetical order is not helpful. You make life much easier for your hosts by arranging delegation lists in strict order of seniority.

The list should be in the order of position — most important person first, least important person last. If it is known, give the translated Chinese name for each guest with surname first.

Additionally, it is useful if the position is given for the most significant delegates, and for any other delegates where they have a formal position. As a mark of respect, people are addressed by their position and then their surname. You will be introduced to Editor Zhuang and his preference would be to address you as Manager Lambert. It's a little old-fashioned but it sends a good message.

It is very helpful if the surnames on the list are printed first and in capitals. This avoids the situation where you are introduced as Mister Bob rather than more correctly, Mister Ellis. When sending a guest list to your Chinese counterparts it is more useful to use this structure — position, surname, name. Government is first, then respected education positions such as professor or master teacher, and then industry. The Chinese side will use this hierarchical list to organise seating and to match appropriate counterparts.

Premier, GILES, Adam (Government)
Director, Asian Relations, DORAN, Brendan (Government)
Master Teacher, GUPPY, Daryl 大师 顾比戴若 (Education)
Executive Director, FAHEY, Stephen (Industry)
General Manager, MARIKA, Janis 总经理 卓曼 (Industry)
Manager, OTHMAN, Norian, (Industry)
YANG NanNan 杨楠楠 (Staff)
CAVANAGH, Michael (Staff)
JENKINS, David (Staff)
TIPPETT, Gordon (Staff)
Translator, CHEN Weili 翻译 陈威立 (Translator)

The reverse also applies. A visiting Chinese delegation will prefer to send a list arranged in strict order of hierarchy. This hierarchical order should be observed when welcoming guests and arranging seating positions at head tables and other tables. Where possible, people of equal position should be seated with each other. Remember the translator is also required to sit near to the person who requires translation services. There is no such thing as free seating — i.e., choosing your own seats — in a Chinese banquet or meeting.

This applies in both China and the West. Correct seating arrangements start with the guest list that has been provided in correct hierarchical order.

Another related issue relates to conference name tags. From a Western perspective the name is the most important feature. From a Chinese perspective, the position, or status, of the person is just as important as the name. The extra ink required to print the position as well as the name on the name tag is not worth quibbling about. The impact of having this additional information is substantial. It enables networking to proceed smoothly and effectively.

Watch when name cards are exchanged at a dinner table. Often, each guest lays them on the table in front as a reference. Not surprisingly the Chinese guests, even those with good English language skills, turn the cards so the Chinese side is up. European guests, including those who read Chinese, turn the cards so the English side is up. This is a simple convenience denied when conference name tags are in English only.

After the meeting, or the meal, is completed it is not unusual to see guests get up and exchange WeChat QR codes with selected people.

## No Free Seating

The purpose of a meeting has an important impact on the seating arrangements in China and it is useful to remember this when meeting with Chinese counterparts, both in China and also when hosting Chinese delegations.

Mention a meeting and most of us imagine a conference room with people gathered around a table. China has introduction — get to know you — meetings and business meetings. The structure of each is different but the seating arrangements run along similar themes.

The introduction meeting is typically a first-time meeting with a general introduction of the people involved. At governmental and departmental level this may take place in a long room. Two chairs are arranged at the end of the room and seats extend down both sides of the room. In Chinese meetings the two most important participants are seated at the head of the room next to each other, often in very large chunky chairs, with a small table between them to hold their cups of tea. These are meetings held with participants sitting side-by-side and it's a different, and sometimes difficult, way to hold a business discussion.

Support staff sit in the chairs along the side of the room. Chinese usually to the left of the Chinese host, and Western staff to the right of the Western delegation leader. The most important people sit closest to the head of the room. The least important staff are furthest away from the leaders. You do not have to know the status of people on the other side of the room. This information is instantly available based on where they sit in the hierarchy. The Chinese side makes the same judgments about you depending on where you sit in this configuration.

This side-by-side arrangement is common in high level meetings where participants are meeting for the first time. This may be CEO to CEO level, or government official to government official. From the Western point of view, we think sitting in comfortable chairs side-by-side signals an unnecessary informality that may be inappropriate for a first meeting. We prefer to save this until later when people have had the time to get to know each other. This is actually in contrast to our preference to immediately start addressing people by first names without regard to title.

From the Chinese perspective, if people sit across from each other in the first meeting they feel this creates an adversarial environment. Sitting side-by-side makes people feel like colleagues and creates a friendlier environment. This is not the same as an informal environment and anyone who has sat in large, chunky, uncomfortable chairs in a Chinese introduction meeting will know this is not informal lounging. Creating a friendly environment is the first step to establishing better relations and the seating arrangements create this first impression.

Additionally, in a more formal interpretation, there is a distinct seating hierarchy. The person sitting with their back to the main door is considered subordinate to the person sitting with their back to the wall. Side-by-side seating overcomes any unintended messages about hierarchy.

Sitting side-by-side allows for a more informal discussion and participants need to turn in their chairs to look at each other. Once the relationship has been established then it is fine to have meetings where people sit across from each other around a table. The foundation of co-operation has already been established.

The side-by-side arrangement is suitable for high level meetings. It is not necessary for business meetings, even initial business meetings, where the details of business arrangements are under discussion. People will want to make notes and refer to documents. If you are offered a side-by-side meeting arrangement in China, it sends an important message about your status and the strategic level of the discussions.

Additional meetings tend to use the across-the-table structure with each side facing each other. Potentially it is a more adversarial structure and unless it is truly a meeting to resolve a conflict, then the assumption of adversarial postures should be avoided. When people have trouble understanding language, they pay more attention and take more clues from body language. Make sure your body language is sending the signals you wish or concealing the signals you do not want to send.

In this structure the most important person sits in the middle. The second most important person sits to his right and the third most important to his left. This hierarchy alternates from left to right until the end of the table is reached. In a large delegation a second row of seats may be added. For the Western side, the seating structure in the second row is less important. However, the Chinese side will observe a hierarchical order in the second-row seating and make similar assumptions about the order of the Western side.

The next time you attend one of these meetings, watch the way the Chinese participants move into the room and directly to their seating. Contrast this with the way your Western colleagues mill about, politely offering and refusing seating positions. If you want to send a clear message about who is responsible for what level of tasks, then the way you choose your seats and where you sit sends a much more powerful message than anything written on a name card.

When hosting delegations or meetings with Chinese in your home country you can choose to send the same message simply by adjusting the seating arrangements.

Step outside of the formal meeting and hosting environment and the challenges of seating remain the same. Unless it is eating with close friends, there is always a seating protocol. Unlike budget airlines, there is never free seating.

## Treaty Foundations

Much has been written about Chinese negotiating styles, so these business bites are small. Recently I had the opportunity to talk with several CEOs who have successful businesses in various parts of China. Amongst other things, we were discussing negotiating styles in China. It quickly became clear there is not just one way of Chinese negotiations. Not surprising when you remember the size of China and the diversity of culture.

In Northern China, the typical negotiation starts with personal trust. The relationship is, in some ways, the most important feature. The negotiation starts with principles of co-operation. Only after they feel both sides share the same principles can the negotiations really begin. This may take months, and many trips, to develop. Then they set out the big points, the framework. Northern Chinese will fight strongly for principle but not always pay so much attention to detail. That's for people lower down the organisation to worry about.

Shanghai is different. Detail is important. Negotiations are tough and discussions can be very straightforward. Once a deal, or agreement signed, it will remain essentially unaltered. If you miss out something in the initial agreement it is very hard to have it included at a later stage. The first offer is never accepted because it is just the starting point of negotiation. Many Westerners feel much more comfortable in this environment because it more closely resembles Western negotiating styles.

Southern China is by far the most difficult area to work in. Misinformation is considered part of a legitimate negotiating strategy. It is often difficult to enforce agreement terms. The CEO with most of his business in Guangzhou described it as an ongoing battle about every dollar. It is all about the money. People who have worked in business in Hong Kong find the direct cut and thrust in Guangzhou more comfortable, but equally, they feel out of place working in Beijing.

Despite these differences in style, there is one uniting factor. The Chinese feel more satisfied with a negotiation if it has involved a long struggle. The struggle develops respect for your adversary and this cuts both ways. Respect is earned and before you treat, it starts with the way you greet, meet and seat.

## The Gift of Giving

Gifts come first but are given last. They are first because much thought is and should be given to the type of gift, its quality, and its symbolism. When possible, it is best to discuss with others on the Chinese side so that the value of the exchanged gifts is about the same. This avoids loss of face if your gift is of a lower or higher standard than the gift given to you.

Gifts fall into four main categories. The first are State gifts representative of the country or province. It's a protocol we are not concerned with in these business bites.

The second are personal gifts, and these can create a problem. If the gift you give as a business gift is also of a personal nature, then the gift may be seen as an invitation to bribery. Great care must be taken to avoid giving this impression as there are very adverse consequences for recipients under the ongoing Tiger and Flies anti-corruption campaign. A business gift should be something suitable for public display and from a Chinese perspective this often includes high quality tea in presentation boxes.

The third are just small tokens of appreciation for staff and delegation members. These include city or state lapel pins or souvenir style gifts.

The fourth are gifts exchanged to open a business relationship. They demonstrate sincerity, intent, and purpose. Deciding what is appropriate is a difficult decision. Where possible work with your Chinese contacts to determine what is appropriate. They will also appreciate working with you in the same way to reach an acceptable exchange that gives face to both parties. This avoids unpleasant surprises.

Gifts give face, and in some circumstances the gifts may be opened in public but only if the type of gift is already known to both parties. In my first conference in Beijing, I gave and received pre-arranged public gifts. I work in financial markets, so my gift was a framed Qing Dynasty bond, issued under the 1898 imperial purple seal. It was a return of a minor historical artefact to China. The gift gave me face and also gave face to the conference hosts. More than a decade later it still hangs in the Chairman's office.

Understand what your choice of gift says about you, your intentions, your sincerity, and your commitment to your Chinese business aspirations. If the gift is treated as ritualistic tokenism then it sends a message that can sour the development of future business.

Unless previously arranged, gifts are not often opened when they are given. This is designed to preserve face. If the gift is inappropriate, then the recipient is not embarrassed. Gifts may be wrapped, usually in red paper, but they are often given in a high-quality paper carry bag. Try to avoid gifts which are difficult to carry on a return flight to China.

Gifts are the last step in the process of meet, greet, seat, and treat because they are usually given at the end of a meeting.

## CHINA BUSINESS BITE

Status is essential in a classless society and respect remains configured along Confucian lines starting with age and position. Recognising the importance of hierarchy eliminates confusion and creates the respect that enhances the business environment. Gifts are part of this process.

# Chapter 10

## THROUGH A GLASS DARKLY

Perception is particularly important in the Chinese environment. Whenever we meet strangers, we make instant and involuntary judgements based on perceptions which may be incorrect or be rooted in experiences which we rarely consciously acknowledge. Most times we get away with these shorthand behaviours, but in China these perceptions serve us less well. It pays to look behind the glass or question the perception, rather than peer through a glass darkly.

Standing in line waiting for a taxi at a 5-star hotel in Beijing, I was aware of a high-level official reception party behind me in the lobby. They were obviously waiting for a guest to arrive.

I watched a taxi pull up and an American business man alight. I knew he was American by his loud voice as he proceeded to argue about the taxi fare. The difference was 30 yuan or about $5 US dollars. The doorman was called to assist in the translation, but it was clear this was a dispute about a minor money matter. The taxi driver got the worse end of the deal and left unsatisfied. The American saved $5, walked through the lobby and met with the official reception party.

I wondered about the future success of his business proposition. Whilst it is good for your reputation in the US to 'pinch pennies', the same behaviour is seen as evidence of financial weakness in China. People need to be confident that the proposed partner is financially sound and arguing about a few dollars does not send the right signal.

I have no idea if the angry penny-pinching American businessman successfully concluded a deal. If he did then I suspect it was on less favourable terms than he would have liked as the Chinese side would be concerned about his poverty-driven approach to costs.

Perceptions work in other ways. We participated at a trade show event and the organisers provided us with translators. The organising committee billed us for a range of costs associated with the event. The fee included translators, business arrangements and other details. The impression created was that these were costs to the organiser and were being passed onto participants. No problem there.

Unfortunately, the perception was not quite correct. The translator came from a Foreign Language University. This was part of her work experience and a component of her course work. She was not paid, although the University may have received a fee.

Our exhibition stand was also staffed by some of our Western office employees who had no Chinese language ability. They relied totally on the translator to interpret for them. No business was possible without the translator. She was the temporary voice of our company. She had done some research on the company and the area we worked in as she was not familiar with our business area. She was, in short, an invaluable part of the team for this event.

Working for free is great for the employer, and for the student she felt the experience was sufficient payment. I see it as type of exploitation, and even more so given the level of dependence we had on the translator's skill and ability. Was the skill of value to us? The answer is clearly yes. Although we may have paid an organisation for the provision of translators, is it appropriate that the translator received no payment? Personally, I am not comfortable with this so I chose to pay the translator by way of a cash gift. It was an acknowledgement of a job well done and it created a favourable perception or impression.

Rich man, poor man? Perceptions count. In China, it often takes very little to make a significant impression, whether positive or negative. My personal preference in this translator situation was to pay the translator a gift, in this case 500 yuan for 2 days of work. It is not a lot for me, but it meant a great deal to the student and perhaps in the future our paths may cross again. It is very much a personal decision, but worth taking the time to think about it.

In working with the Chinese, it is remarkably easy to misinterpret situations, if we continue to hold onto our cultural preconceptions which are so often based on misinformation. Western journalists often comment with disdain on the Chinese practice of giving red packets to journalists who attend press briefings. It's unethical they claim. A Western journalist friend relates a tale of a Western PR person who invited Chinese journalists to an event where free food and drinks were supplied — the standard Western practice — but nobody turned up. Unbelievable, she writes, who would expect journalists would turn down free food and drink? Of course, free food and drink are the direct Western equivalent of a Chinese red packet but apparently only one of these poses an ethical problem or carries an implied hint of corruption.

Misunderstandings come from the most basic observations and they serve as a warning when we try to interpret events in a foreign environment. One Western author spending a placement in Shanghai has two young children. When walking in the local park she met many people, all of whom, she concluded, seemed to be commenting on the fact that she had two children. "They hold up two fingers and point to the children" she writes. Her conclusion was that it represented a "V for victory sign" and they "were actually congratulating her on the success in having two children because of the strict one child policy in China".

Perhaps it did not occur to her that if she had three children, people would hold up three fingers in sign language to confirm the number. When I walk into a restaurant in China with friends, I will ask for a table for six — *liu wei* 六位 — and hold up my hand in the Western symbol for telephone with fingers clenched, thumb up and little finger extended. It's a sign for telephone in the Western parlance, but represents the number six in the Chinese lexicon of hand signals.

This type of duality in China means the simple is often impossibly frustrating and the seemingly impossible often turns out to be quite simple. Much of this apparent contradiction comes from misunderstandings that come from different ways of thinking and not just expression. I was reminded of this as I was strolling in the garden with a friend through a block of apartments. In the West, the path between these buildings would be a straight line. In China, the path is always curved, with twists and bends.

It's a perfect metaphor for the differences in thinking. This becomes particularly important when trying to explain or resolve a problem. Resolution is always complicated by language. What we understand a word to mean is not the same understanding that our Chinese partner has. It important to locate these 'common' word misunderstandings very quickly because they can lead to significantly different interpretations of the same event or agreement. Unless caught quickly, going down this road leads to contractual disaster.

Be alert also for words that are used in place of our common expressions. A request for someone to investigate a problem is acceptable. A request to solve the problem, or fix the problem, or find a solution to the problem is not likely to give the result you want. The difference? I can investigate a problem and not find a solution, and still have face.

Surmounting the language misunderstandings does not always solve the problem. Straight-line thinking is often not readily accepted and, in some cases, it is seen as offensive and impolite.

Problems are approached from many different angles. The central issues are returned to again and again. This aspect of 'touching base' and 'revisiting' matters that in a Western sense have been discussed and resolved, is frustrating and irritating. But it is part of the process. It's the meandering Chinese path rather than the Western straight line bulldozed through all obstacles.

It's a lengthy process designed to consider all the relevant material, to test each step before moving onto another. It is not a frivolous exercise, because once the decision is made, and the problem resolved, it is cast in stone to a greater degree than the decisions reached by straight line bulldozing.

These are notes on Chinese thinking, so it is appropriate to loop back and finish near where we began. A Western landscape designer who uses curved paths soon finds his design is defeated by Western thinking habits. The park users blaze new paths across the gardens, always in a straight line from point A to point B. The next time you choose to leave the path and take a direct short cut across the park, remember how this is a product of Western thinking.

Our perceptions of appropriate public or private behaviour are also challenged by different belief and value systems. I am a writer, and in China this has unexpected consequences. Every week I write many articles, including financial and economic analysis for Shanghai Security News and China Global Television Network digital. I also write financial market analysis notes for CNBC and our own newsletters. But not all writing is work-related and this yields some unexpected benefits.

In September, I was once again walking with friends and a business colleague in Xiang Shan, the mountain park near Beijing. By happenstance we ended up near a grove of bamboo where we had rested once before several years previously. At the time, I had jotted down some notes which I developed into a short poem based on the Tang Dynasty poetry structure. Later on, I had tentatively sent it to my friend. She was delighted and passed it on to our business colleague.

Chinese conversation is sprinkled with references to Tang and Song Dynasty poetry, and to the classics like the *Dream of the Red Mansions* and *The Romance of the Three Kingdoms*. Many people write poetry, or practise calligraphy or aspire to playing the *gu zheng* 古筝, a classical Chinese musical instrument developed in the Tang dynasty. It is a sign of learning and it is greatly valued. My accidental poem added an additional dimension to my friendship and the business relationship. Seated again by the same bamboo grove I was asked if I would write poetry again.

China values culture and the Confucius ideal of a 'gentleman' in a way that we do not in the West. There is a higher value placed on academic qualifications whereas we are often dismissive of this, preferring to substitute it with experience and hard knocks from the University of Life. Learning and age is more respected in China, so there are advantages in emphasising these features in a way that would not be appropriate in a Western environment.

You do not have to become a poet, but if you have a less publicised desire to listen to opera, to read the classics, to walk in the park — not a vigorous endurance hike — and appreciate nature, to paint or to recite Walt Whitman or Banjo Patterson, then China is the place to bring this into the business relationship. It may deliver unexpected benefits.

Westerners looking for business in China are commonplace. Westerners speaking passable or good Chinese are more common than they used to be. Westerners who can write in Chinese are much rarer and this radically alters perceptions. In the initial contract discussions for publishing my first financial market book in China, we met with senior executives. At the beginning of the meeting we were told they had another meeting at 1 pm, capping our available time and, for them and us, saving face when they left after a short meeting.

For this meeting I did not speak Chinese and my colleague Chen Jing did an excellent presentation. She explained how the translation would be localised for Chinese market conditions. The executives were not particularly impressed and as we all stood up it was clear that there was little inclination to proceed. At the conclusion of the meeting I gave a gift copy of my English book to the CEO. I asked if he would like me to sign it for him and he nodded agreement.

Taking back the book, I wrote in poorly executed Chinese characters, *jiao yi cheng gong* 交易成功 trade with success, and signed my name in both English and Mandarin characters. I gave the book back to him. He politely opened the book, looked at my signature, then recoiled in surprise. "Sit down", he directed his staff who were already standing and ready to leave. The publishing contract was finalised in the next 30 minutes and the other 1 pm meeting forgotten. Writing in Chinese changed perceptions dramatically because it indicated a greater commitment to working in China.

Business in China is too important to unknowingly get off on the wrong foot simply by arguing over a few dollars with a taxi driver, or assuming that two fingers deliver a political message compatible with your preconceptions. First impressions do count. Historically, Chinese have regarded Westerners as barbarians largely because of their lack of cultured behaviour. Like it or not, this is an historical preconception we have to overcome when we do business with China. This is a behind-the-border barrier but there are many simple methods we can use to break down the barrier. If we do not recognise the barrier in the first place then we cannot take action to break it down. Success in China is about making more effective use of our strengths and minimising our weakness to improve the quality of the business we do, in and with China. We often see China through a glass darkly, so the challenge is to search for better methods of illumination.

When ignorance is confirmed by preconceptions then common sense goes out the window and this serves as a warning to all who aim to work in China or with the Chinese. It is easy to eat with chopsticks, but it is not useful if your understanding of China is limited to a knife and fork approach. It's a danger we all face in working in any foreign environment and overcoming this is a significant business challenge in China. China shakes the very foundations of consumer commerce and that can be either a threat or an opportunity.

## CHINA BUSINESS BITE

Everything you do in China is closely scrutinised because of the potential for confusion and for clues to your character. The perception you create for others in the first 30 seconds of a meeting is either an essential foundation or a pothole. It's your choice and you rarely get a second chance.

# Chapter 11

## SMILING FOR CASH

Whilst in Beijing I needed cash, so I smiled at an ATM and it gave me money. Facial recognition is now enabled for China bank accounts and ATMs have been upgraded. This service follows on the AliPay "Smile to Pay" campaign that was launched in 2018. It uses reliable facial recognition technology to verify payments rather than a pin code and is just part of a digital economy where the use of physical cash is rapidly fading. At a modern juice bar in Xi'an, I was unable to pay for a drink with cash. I had to use WePay.

The adoption of facial recognition by Chinese banks underpins just how advanced, secure and reliable facial recognition technology has become in China. It is just one waypoint on China's digital highway construction that has been accelerated by COVID.

This is in contrast to many Western examples of facial recognition software that have an irritatingly low success rate when applied to Caucasians and an appallingly low success race with other groups. It is in stark contrast to banking systems in the United States that continues to rely on credit cards with magnetic strips, or even Australian systems with embedded chips and easily hackable four-digit passwords. China is a digital economy we cannot afford to dismiss nor ignore.

Outside my hotel in Beijing is a cluster of roadside stalls selling everything from fresh fruit, BBQ *yang rou chuan* 羊肉 — lamb skewers and as the weather is getting colder, freshly roasted sweet potatoes cooked over a modified discarded oil drum. These are one-man, one-cart operators who may or may not be licensed food vendors. They are the very lowest rung of business operators and definitely outside the tax and banking system.

Yet many of them offer the most sophisticated web-based payment systems. I pay for my home-made hawthorn paste, or buy hot chestnuts for a few yuan and pay using my handphone. They are all on WeChat and all accept WePay.

This is a revolution that Western banks and systems are unaware of. Let's look at some of the features and compare them to what we experience in this area of internet payments and transactions.

- Transaction size has no minimum. Buy one sweet potato for one yuan or a dozen. It makes no difference.
- There are no greedy transaction fees.
- WeChat does not take a slice of every transaction so it makes it possible to enable low value transactions.
- There is no barrier to entry. No minimum business size, no complex forms and intrusive registration process.
- There is no set up fee. Unlike Western bank operated transaction services there is no monthly fee just for the right to have a terminal sitting on your shop counter.

This internet transaction model is very different from the US-based model like ApplePay which are bank look-a-likes with their host of transaction, registration and participation fees. That's not true e-commerce. It is just another iteration of the banking transaction system using better technology.

But it's not just my neighbourhood fruit seller. I needed to arrange for a chauffeured car to take some conference delegates 200 kilometres from Qingdao to Rizhao. How to pay? The company does not accept international credit cards. The old way required a telegraphic transfer for the hire car deposit. Very high bank fees, unfavourable exchange rates with very wide spreads and delays of up to three days before payment is received. If I had been able to pay by international credit card I would have been hit with all of the above and a 3.5% commission fee on the value of the transaction. It's a gravy train for bank profits and an excessive expense for business.

The solution? Draw on funds in my WeChat account and pay by WePay over the internet. Quick, efficient, inexpensive, secure; doing business was a pleasure. A transaction revolution is taking place in China and it is being rapidly exported. There is no excuse for your businesses not to offer this payment service, particularly for Chinese tourists.

COVID has increased the update of the so-called digital economy in Western countries but they remain a long way behind China. Understanding the size of this gap is a first step towards doing effective business in China.

Valentine's Day, Mother's Day and Father's Day all have their origins in slick marketing campaigns designed to boost retail sales. The merry red Santa Claus we are so familiar with started life as an advertising idea from Coca Cola.

China joined the fray with Singles Day and if you haven't heard of it then you are missing a 20 billion USD one-day shopping bonanza.

November 11 is written as 11/11. This collection of single 1s makes this China's Singles Day. Singles Day started in China during the early 1990s and was billed as a day for young people without partners to get together, go to a Karaoke club, or head out on a collective shopping spree. It's the shopping that prompted internet giant, Alibaba, to start offering Singles Day special discounts on Taobao and T-mall, in 2009. The rest, as they say, is history.

Recent singles day sales have topped 20 billion dollars in sales in a single day. Transaction peaked at 86,000 sales per second. China Post delivered 760 million packages as a result of the online shopping frenzy.

Chinese consumers use the Singles Day sale as an excuse to buy almost anything from television sets to cheaper groceries. There is also a focus on goods from overseas, with European and Australian holidays, milk products and European wine featuring amongst the online deals.

There are two aspects of this buying frenzy that deserve notice. First is the sheer numbers, vibrancy and sophistication of the online market in China. E-commerce in all its retail forms is far more advanced and competitive than anywhere outside of China. The Black Friday sales in the US — the equivalent of China's Singles Day — clocked up a measly 1.8 billion dollars.

The use of e-commerce has been a major factor in spurring the improvement of Chinese logistics services, including the humble China Post. I can send a 6 kg package from Guangzhou to Dalian — from one end of China to the other — in 2 days for around $8 using China's SF courier service. SF stands for Shun Feng in Chinese, which literally means to go with the wind, but I think it stands for Super-Fast in English. It's a service that leaves many of its Western competitors in China languishing in the dust.

The second aspect revolves around a key question. Why is your company not involved in this market? True, there are barriers to the bulk supply of goods and services, but they are being overcome by foreign companies.

Metcash, the company behind IGA supermarkets, recently set up a site on Alibaba's T-mall platform. The group timed its entry to the online Chinese market so that it would be up and running for the Singles Day sale. It has a team of 21 full-time staff based in Shanghai doing product sourcing, sales and market research.

One of the key advantages of the online market is the ability to offer high quality premium products in limited quantities. We cannot all be a Metcash, particularly in the SME sector where businesses tend to be smaller. But there are opportunities for smaller businesses to offer products into this active and mobile market. This includes holiday package offers, discounted accommodation, tours and sales of specialist items.

Just as every business should have a WeChat account, they should also have a presence on Taobao. If you are not there then your 95 million potential customers simply do not know you exist.

Despite oft-repeated Western concerns about a slowing Chinese economy, this is a rapidly expanding consumer market. Higher disposal incomes have led to higher rates of consumption. The massive growth in international tourism with Chinese citizens travelling overseas is a clear indication of changing consumption patterns based on confidence in the future.

The astounding value of transactions with the Singles Day sales underlines a new propensity to consume and settle the transaction in new ways. The challenge for your business is to get onto this sales channel. That starts, in part, by developing a presence on platforms like Singles Day and Chinese social media like WeChat.

This digital trade and commerce highway is already open and it is part of the New Silk Road discussed in the next section. We can choose whether we want to drive on the highway, or stay on slower secondary roads which use different standards and protocols. The choices are more urgent for Western countries because much of their export trade is with countries already using this digital highway.

Indonesia's National Single Window (INSW) Customs clearance program is part of this China-inspired highway and replaces a cumbersome, time-consuming and corruption-friendly process that relied on multiple bits of paper spread across multiple official desks. Australia is aware of INSW but is not participating. Participating in INSW can deliver immediate benefits to Australian exporters to Indonesia, and to other countries in Asia as the INSW template is rolled out.

However, if we don't know the highway exists, or reject using it for non-commercial reasons, then we cut ourselves out of trade and commercial opportunities. Engagement with China and with other countries in Asia which trade with China, rests upon the ability to develop and deploy compatible technology to work with these advanced digital systems. This is a choice the United States seems determined to frustrate by attacking Chinese tech companies like Huawei and TenCent. These attacks force business to make uncomfortable and uncommercial decisions.

The new Silk Road is a digital road and it is of such importance that China President Xi Jinping has overseen a government study on innovation, blockchain and digital currency. China already has a leading role in its development and has integrated blockchain in various state-owned or managed sectors such as customs, healthcare, and banking. The 'Smile to Pay" service at my local Beijing bank ATM is one aspect of this progress.

The multilateral trade system on which SMEs rely, is increasingly safeguarded by building a digital currency alternative to the dollar-based trade settlement system. This means free trade and cross-border transactions cannot be threatened or hijacked by unilateral decisions to deny access to the SWIFT settlement system and the system of US-based co-respondent banks.

China's central bank's digital currency project has the highest profile, but we cannot ignore the deep integration of blockchain in artificial intelligence, big data, and the internet of things. Already, smart cities, transportation, energy, employment, medical health, commodity anti-counterfeiting, and food safety are all actively using blockchain.

It is easier to access this New Silk Road market, to sell digital innovation into this market, to transact cross-border trade in this market, if we acknowledge and adhere to the development standards. We need a licence to drive on this digital highway and like it or not, it's a Chinese licence.

That poses a trade dilemma. Do we back Western blockchain applications that may be incompatible with the standards applied to the more advanced China implementation? The answer is the difference between efficient trade clearances and product sales, and ships waiting at the end of the line to unload. The answer is the difference between software applications that are compatible with the standards of our major Asian trading partners, and software applications that are built on an incompatible structure. Those who acknowledge and adopt these Chinese digital standards can keep smiling and money will come.

## CHINA BUSINESS BITE

E-commerce is not a concept in China, it is an everyday reality. Business success is improved when we use and apply these standards and protocols.

# Chapter 12

## CHINESE CURIOSITIES

A chop, or stone carved seal with your name, is a popular cheap tourist souvenir from Asia, purchased as a curiosity. The chop is not a curiosity in China. It is an essential part of business.

In China the chop is an essential tool for signing documents, approving company transactions and managing Chinese business. These are not the pretty tourists chops, but officially issued chops and there is only one for each company.

In most Western countries, the signature on a document makes the document legal and binding. Not so in China. A Chinese signature on a document means nothing in terms of Chinese law. The company must also chop all contacts, invoices, meeting minutes and other legal documents.

The person who holds the chop thus holds a great deal of power. Cheques for instance are valid when they are chopped. A signature is not necessary. This is particularly important for Western companies who must leave their chop in China. It's essential to ensure the chop is entrusted to safe and reliable hands.

The chop is also used in a multi-page contract to ensure no pages are missing, or inserted at a later date. The contract pages are fanned out and then the chop is applied across the fan so that each page has a partial imprint of the chop on it. It is very easy to see if any pages are missing. The full chop is then applied to the final page where signatures would normally go.

Documents and contracts designed to be used in China and also outside China should be chopped and signed by both parties. From a

Chinese perspective, the document is legally binding if it has the company chop and your chop. From a Western perspective the document is legal and binding if it has your signature and a signature from the Chinese counter party. Ensuring the document has signatures from all parties and chops from all parties helps to avoid problems in the future.

Many countries no longer require company seals or chops. However, if you are intending to do business in China it is very useful to make sure you have a company chop with you. The chop may have no validity in your home country — your signature carries that validity — but the company chop will be readily accepted and recognised by your Chinese counterparts. Make sure the chop is always used with red ink. Business service centres in hotels will always have a pad of red stamp ink available.

It is also useful to remember when submitting invoices for payment by a Chinese company that these invoices must also be chopped before they are regarded as valid. It is a difficult process if you are claiming airfares issued over the internet, but they can be validated with a chop from the travel agency.

If you are claiming expenses incurred in China then an officially chopped *shang ye fa piao* 商业发票, or more commonly called a *fa piao* 发票 must be presented. Make sure you ask for one when you check out of the hotel as the standard hotel paperwork will not be recognised for reimbursement claims.

Chinese workers do not have the same leave entitlements as generally accepted in the West. The result is a much greater reliance on public holidays and on the generosity of the company.

The Chinese public holidays are:

**New Year's Day** is a one-day holiday on January 1. It may provide a 3-day holiday if it butts onto a weekend.

**Spring Festival,** or the Chinese New Year as it is known in the West is 3 days, but it is often turned into a 9-day holiday — 5 working days and 2 weekends. The date is set by the astrological calendar so it is usually late January to mid-February. It is common for workers to add extra days to this leave period in a futile attempt to beat the rush to get seating on trains and planes so they may return home.

**Qing Ming Festival.** This is a 1-day holiday. The date is set by the astrological calendar and it may provide a 3-day holiday if it butts onto a weekend. Usually in early April.

**May Day/Labour day.** This is May 1. It may provide a 3-day holiday if it butts onto a weekend. If it falls on a Tuesday, then many businesses will close on the Monday and give a 4-day holiday. This extended holiday is at the discretion of individual businesses.

**Dragon Boat Festival.** Also known as Poets day in China. This is a 1-day holiday. The date is set by the astrological calendar and it may provide a 3-day holiday if it butts onto a weekend. This is in June.

**Mid-Autumn Festival** or Mooncake Festival. This is a 1-day holiday. The date is set by the astrological calendar and it may provide a 3-day holiday if it butts onto a weekend. Usually mid to late September.

**National Day Holiday.** This is October 1 to 3 and is often referred to as Golden Week. It may provide a 9-day holiday if it butts onto a weekend. More importantly, it may provide a one-week holiday if the Mid-Autumn Festival falls in late September.

In terms of annual leave there is a guarantee of 5 to 15 days paid annual leave. However annual leave entitlements are growing, particularly in the middle class and professional jobs. Annual leave may be accumulated and taken in a lump, particularly for government workers. Long service leave is 5 working days (from 1 to 9 years seniority), 10 working days (from 10 to 19), 15 working days (from 20 years onwards). The application to private industry is uneven.

Students and teachers have summer and winter holidays for about three months. The summer school holidays generally start around July 1 and end around August 31. The winter school holidays usually fall in January or February, depending on the date of the Spring Festival.

Public holidays represent the only real leave many people have. These are periods of intense travel activity. For business travellers to China, these are times to avoid because your business contacts will be away.

The upper middle class is increasingly accessing paid and unpaid leave more easily. This is driving an increase in demand for independent travel outside the official holiday periods. These numbers are substantial and growing.

Official sponsored business development days are an important additional 'unofficial' holiday for many people. This is where a company or department will travel to a holiday location for training or group activities. This is often for a week. It is common to arrange this as domestic travel to destinations such as Dalian and Hainan. This is a hangover from earlier periods when there were fewer public holidays. It is less common for this to include international travel. However, many international business delegations include a component that reflects this domestic tradition. Some delegates may be only loosely connected with the primary purpose of the delegation.

For many, the Chinese working year has 13 salary months. This extra pay month falls at the start of Spring Festival where it is often expected that employers will provide *hong bao* 红包 — a red packet — to recognise each worker's contribution during the year. It's a bonus for unpaid overtime and worker contributions to the organisation. In service companies, this is often the equivalent of a month's pay. Bonus levels vary from industry to industry but one thing is certain; failure to pay acceptable levels of *hong bao* prior to the Spring Festival often results in workers not returning after the holidays.

This practice developed as compensation for poor wages and conditions in the past. It may not be so relevant now, but many workers and staff expect this and budget for this as a type of holiday pay. As a Western company in China, you may decide if this is necessary. Our preference is to budget for this cost and meet expectations.

## CHINA BUSINESS BITE

Limited holidays are supplemented by company sponsored business development excursions. Overtime is recognised with Hong Bao 13th month payments for staff before Spring Festival. All business is legalised with a chop, not a signature.

# Chapter 13

# CHINA CASE STUDY — COURTING
# THE DRAGON

'Let's attract Chinese investment' is not a plan. It may be an aspiration but getting from the aspiration to a plan and then to results is a long process. It takes a lot more than just a statement of intent to effectively court the dragon. The most effective solution is when the Chinese come to you rather than you go to them. It transfers the balance of power in the relationship. It is often a strategy of 'Tossing Out a Brick to Get Jade'. Creating the situation where they come to you with an offer to invest requires skill and builds on the basic principles discussed below.

These China case study notes summarise some of the key issues involved in attracting Chinese investment. They start with strategic objectives and then investigate how these may be achieved in a practical way. These notes are based on one of our workshop units we deliver via www.workingwithChina.com

The overall strategic objective is to raise your profile so China knows you are open for investment. This may be investment at a state-wide level, or investment into a project, or searching for a buy-out partner to expand your business. Strategy involves four areas:

- People rules
- Talk small, listen big
- Face
- Develop strategic understanding

The learning curve is steep and the road is very unforgiving. How much you get right defines the difference between co-operation, competition or conquest.

## People Rule 1

People trust individuals, not positions. China is not a country with the same ideas of the rule of law as they apply in the West. We are accustomed to the rule of law — an independent body of judgements that does not change. In China, contract protection does not come from a team of lawyers. It comes from people. The application and interpretation of the law changes depending on people. When government leaders change, policy and policy implementation changes.

The emphasis in genuine Chinese business is on relationships. If you cannot rely on the law to protect you then you just make sound judgement about the people you are dealing with. Hence the importance of relationships or *guanxi*.

## People Rule 2

*Guanxi* 关系 and *hao peng you* 好朋友 are the foundation of China business. The terms *guanxi* and *hao peng you* are often poorly understood but they are vital to doing business in China. These concepts are all unavoidable in doing business.

*Guanxi* is loosely translated as relationships. This is usually among family and business friends and is essential for living in China because bureaucracy is so large. When there are millions of people, there are potentially millions of possible mistakes, so you must choose your friends, associates and business associates very carefully. Guanxi helps by providing trusted introductions.

*Hao peng you* translates to good friend. The concept takes on particular meaning for people who experienced aspects of the cultural revolution either as young adults or children. It has meaning in a society with an active public security bureau. There is a level of mistrust and suspicion in many everyday activities that is not experienced as a background environment in the West so good friends take on an additional significance of protection and trust.

This leads to a constant need to re-test and confirm the strength of the relationship, particularly in the early years. Respect these requests and make them work for you.

Assume that inside information is available to the other side in any negotiation and that significant information will be withheld from you, and even from the people you are negotiating with. It is not a unique situation or some dark Chinese conspiracy. It is not much different from the way the float managers sold the highly inflated Facebook IPO to investors in 2012 based on information withheld from the general public.

## People Rule 3

In a classless society class is everything. There are many 'small' people so only 'big' people get business cards and only really important people exchange WeChat connections. You cannot always tell the difference, so you will need a translator or skilled Chinese manager to assist in the navigation of this minefield. The main leaders are not involved in business discussions. They appear only to 'rubber stamp' the final agreement. This also creates an atmosphere of deniability for the actions of juniors. If you are the main leader in your company and also involved in these early discussions then avoid giving what may be seen as undeniable commitments.

This deniability is also a cultural revolution hangover. People paid with their lives for seemingly insignificant decisions so decision making can be extremely slow. This is why we spend so much time in casual discussion — not formal US style negotiations — because it smooths the way, and allows for development of acceptable conditions before formal agreement is reached. It is important to create the time for informal discussions outside of the meeting room.

All significant Chinese businesses interacting with foreign business activities in China are related to government business. Any Chinese business with full government colour, or strong government colour is stable and effective. The rest carry political and sovereign risk.

## Talk Small, Listen Big

Small talk *is* the business and every conversation is important. In the early stages of business discussions there is no such thing as small talk. You are under constant evaluation and this also builds towards contract agreement. Be careful of saying 'Yes' when you mean 'Yes, I will consider it and possibly reject it'. There is no such thing as an unimportant conversation. Everything is weighed carefully with an eye to developing a full relationship. Assume everyone around you understands English, even if they cannot speak it, so keep the small talk to matters of less consequence.

The West prefers a business decision-making model based on vigorous debate. The idea is to let all sides fight in a robust discussion and the best will emerge. This is the purpose of a meeting.

The Chinese model is to find the middle way in quiet discussion before the formal meeting. This is the purpose behind walking with your hosts around Nan Hai in Beijing, or along the Bund in Shanghai. Make time in your scheduling for this to happen. The tour of the tourist spots is not a break from business, it is the business. When the time comes for the formal meeting, everyone knows the solutions so it all appears to be 'rubber stamped'.

The need to avoid confrontation is tied up with many other factors. Usually, this is implemented with some flimsy excuse. It is inconvenient, or the person you need to talk to is on leave and we don't know when he is coming back. Recognise all of these as the polite ways of saying 'No'. Use this method yourself to politely say 'No'. Couch your response in terms of 'Perhaps'.

In desperation, Chinese people may simply say 'Yes' to shut you up because they believe saying 'No' would cause offence. It means you missed the inconvenient signals. A 'Yes' can actually mean 'No' if you push too hard for it.

## Off Your Face

Face, as mentioned previously in Chapter 3, is a complicated concept. In practical terms, a loss of face is whenever your Chinese counterpart feels even mildly embarrassed because this disturbs the harmony of the relationship. When you lose face, this may be signalled by nervous laughter behind hands — they are embarrassed on your behalf.

In China face operates every day at every level. It is a minefield, even in small talk. It is difficult to think in this way, so just be extra polite and be guided by the behaviour of your Chinese counterparts. Of course, there are ignorant and impolite Chinese people — but they are not the people you are doing business with.

Everybody has a job and no matter how unimportant this gives face. In the West we assume people do many tasks. We are proud of our multi-tasking. In China people have one task, and the rest is done by others. It takes time for things to filter down the chain. It is important to identify who is in the chain, at what level, and what task they can do.

Everybody is happy to be courted by Westerners with expense accounts, but this does not mean they are the right persons you want to talk to. Use a local translator who is able to recognise who is important. This is recognised by seating arrangements, by positioning at meetings and by the order of introductions. We don't have these skills. It is very desirable that your translator should have them but as a rule of thumb, younger translators do not have these skills.

The meal is about relationship building. It is not about enjoyment or relaxation and it is not about formal business. Save your relaxation for when you return home. Debrief in your room, not in the lobby.

For Westerners a business meal is where the deal is done. In China, the business meal is where they decide if they will or will not do business with you. The deal is done in the informal talks that we often consider to be inconsequential small talk, so we are really surprised when this small talk comes back to bite us.

## Off Your Face 2

It is estimated that most of us use about 1,000 words in daily conversation. To read basic Chinese to lower middle school standard requires a vocabulary of around 3,000 individual characters. All of these must be memorised and understood immediately on sight. Chinese memorisation and recall skills are astounding by Western standards.

This difference is seen in meetings. Your team takes extensive notes of the meeting. Their team takes almost no notes at all, or if they do, it's often more likely to be observational notes. They are trying to work out who has the real power. Three months later an issue comes up, and the Chinese side will quote you verbatim. Check your minutes, and you will find they are accurate!

Expect your counterparts to have a good memory of every miscommunicated intention and every unintentional insult. This leads to loss of face, erosion of trust and suddenly everything becomes inconvenient. Add alcohol to this mix and it can be lethal.

Many Westerners think drinking is about macho efforts to show who can be the last man standing. Many Chinese believe drunks reveal their true character and we have this same belief in the West. We know mild people who turn into aggressive drunks and the reserved girl who becomes a giggly drunk. We pass this off as an incidental outcome, but for the Chinese this is a very important aspect of business drinking.

Our Chinese hosts may also be drunk, or appear to be drunk, but consider two things. First of all, their drunken conversation was in Chinese and you didn't understand a word. Second, your drunken conversation was in English and every one of their translators understood every word because they were not drinking.

## Strategic Understanding

The Chinese understanding of the concept of a joint venture is different from the West. They think joint ventures are about people, then organisation, and perhaps the law. This is why a Chinese contract is a starting document, not an ending document. We think a joint venture is about law and organisations and lastly people. These cultural differences are an obstacle to doing Western style business in China. It is an obstacle to doing business our way, but we can do business the Chinese way if we can understand these differences.

It is also difficult for Chinese people to deal with the business and political structure in China. They have frustrations with processes just as Western business find the processes a confusing labyrinth. We need to identify what works in China and not complain about how much easier it is to do business at home. What appears easy is often very difficult, but what appears impossible may also be unexpectedly easy.

One thing for certain: China will no longer be at the mercy of foreign powers. They are determined never to let the fall of the Qing dynasty repeat itself. Examine your every proposal and action through this filter and you can do business in China.

China is too large for a blanket campaign, so identify and target partners/interests. Road shows and trade shows raise profile, but delegations are more effective when they are armed with specific proposals. Identify the right people and build relationships. Start with attending international China trade expos and use these to identify the right people and then bring them to your home country. Business involving significant foreign exchange or investment requires Chinese Government colour for smooth success so do not avoid companies with government connections on the grounds that they are not true models of business.

Bring key people to your country but provide a high standard of hosting. Ensure there is time for informal small talk because this time is when real business is done. Expect requests for unrelated favours. These are a store from which you can withdraw in the future for return assistance in resolving complications in China.

If you have the budget then employ a local representative just for relationship development skills. This is a soft skill in the West, but it is absolutely essential in China. Provide media material that has been translated in China because contemporary mainland language usage is essential. Translations done in Hong Kong or by overseas Chinese do not reflect mainland usage so you lose face and credibility.

## CHINA BUSINESS BITE

The facts are different in China so learn how business is done the China way.

# Chapter 14

# CHINA CASE STUDY — TRADE EXHIBITION ORGANISATION

Working in a foreign environment has its frustrations. Working in China has its own particular set of frustrations, not least because the 'last minute' was invented in China. I have had the pleasure of working with a number of foreign companies in China in event organisation and management at trade expos, sometimes as a partner, and sometimes as an exhibitor. The conference teams I work with are highly skilled and excellent at their jobs. They are professional and are experienced in running international events. In many cases the teams also speak Chinese. But China has, at times, had them pulling out their hair in frustration.

The problems they experience are common and we look at 10 of the problems most frequently mentioned. This is not intended as criticism. Use this to anticipate areas of difficulty when you are next involved as an event organiser, or as an exhibitor, or when you decide to purchase a booth at a trade expo in Shanghai. Where possible we also look at the potential reasons for these problems, and also some potential solutions as suggested by the organisers. To keep a balance, we also look at the things these skilled conference organisers love about working in China.

These are not problems unique for foreign exhibitors. These problems are equally frustrating to all exhibitors and organisers.

**1. The Chinese partners constantly going back on their word without prior notification. This makes planning very**

**challenging, especially when it involves promises we have made to our guests and clients. This is the most significant problem.** Some examples of this include:

a) VIP seats agreed upon can be withdrawn without notification on the day of the event.
b) The exhibition area allocated at the initial planning stage was changed and the change forced upon us.
c) Agreed to bring government officials to tour the exhibition area but did not deliver on the promise
d) Agreed to put company names on exhibitor passes but did not do this.
e) Promises to provide exhibitor passes but then claimed there were insufficient passes.

## POTENTIAL REASONS

Decisions made at the top level are not always passed down correctly to lower levels. China has a maze of bureaucracy, and this applies particularly to any event organised in conjunction with a government office.

People may appear to 'go back on their word' when a polite refusal has been misinterpreted as a 'yes'. This is a common problem when Westerners are involved in these arrangements. Ask the same question in several different ways and find a consistent answer. This helps nail down commitment and prevents misunderstanding.

Government officials have minds of their own in every country. They respond to a wide range of other influences so these offers should always be treated with caution unless arranged at an official government to government protocol level and even then, there can be last minute changes.

Seating at VIP areas is always a contentious issue involving face. The order of seating is very important. Seats may be withdrawn simply because somebody forgot to print the place names for the seats. A block of seats may be withdrawn because the guest list provided created confusion.

Of course, the reason may also be that the status of your involvement has slipped further down the list of priorities.

## POTENTIAL SOLUTIONS

Identify the chain of command. Where possible, problems should be raised and solved from the top down. Do not expect a problem to be reported and raised up the command structure. Where possible, work with those who are giving the instructions rather than those who are following instructions.

One organiser said they did fight back and kicked up a big fuss with the higher management. They finally got their way, but they also worried they had offended some people along the way.

Distinguish between a firm commitment, a polite commitment and a commitment conditional upon the agreement of other people, such as a politician or official. Develop alternative plans for those commitments which are not firm.

Check the details, such as passes, frequently. This type of detail disappears easily in the Chinese bureaucracy where there is often a person for every single aspect of a job. It is time consuming, so factor this into the event planning. Where possible, arrive early so these last minute problems can be resolved.

Where possible, write into contract agreements the right to withhold a portion of payment if costs have been transferred to you such as emergency printing of passes.

When seating arrangements are suddenly changed, or disappear, try to establish the true reason. This may include not having printed the place names for the seating. In this case, offer to provide these and have them ready on standby. It may be due to the list you provided which listed people alphabetically rather than by order of importance. Somebody recognised that the CEO's name was halfway down the list. This created confusion, so it was easier to simply withdraw all the seats. It is assumed any list will include the most important person at the top and the least important person at the bottom.

If the status of your involvement in the event has slipped further down the list of priorities then unfortunately you have very few options.

## 2. Government officials very bureaucratic. Very long approval process, even for simple matters such as whether we can have one tiny spot at registration counter on the day of the event.

### POTENTIAL REASONS

Although it's a French word, the French did not invent bureaucracy. This is an original Chinese invention and the idea of red tape has a long history in China. Red ribbon — what we call tape — was used to bind official documents in China. It is exacerbated by the meticulous division of responsibility. A single bureaucrat may be responsible for a very small area, and he will have to co-ordinate with multiple other bureaucrats over what appear to be easy-to-resolve issues.

In some areas, reluctance to make a decision comes about because people do not want to carry the responsibility for the decision. This is particularly so if you have made the request to the wrong person. The person may lose face if he says he can do something and then finds he cannot, so it's simpler for him to say it is inconvenient or to avoid taking action. Others may be worried about the consequences of making the decision, even though it appears to be a small issue from our perspective.

It's a small comfort, but it is not specifically directed at you. Chinese people experience exactly the same delays, confusion, countermanding orders and frustration. The lower the government official you are dealing with, the slower the process becomes. Unfortunately, as a Westerner you are often locked into working with the lowest person in the decision-making chain.

### POTENTIAL SOLUTIONS

The Chinese overcome this problem wherever possible with *guanxi*. You cannot buy this. It is built on a network of friends, contacts, shared friendships. You can however tap into these networks on an informal basis by employing people who do have these contacts. It is easy to be misled into believing people have more contacts than they really have, so care is required. Look at the costs of using an on-site consultancy team to do some of this drudgery work. It will cost money, but this is counter balanced by the time savings and the reduction of frustration.

It is also useful to remember your own face. As logistics organisers in the West, we are accustomed to taking on many of the smaller tasks on the principle that we all pitch in and lend a hand. Not so in China. Here the principle is that you add another staff member to do the legwork. If you do the work, then you take this work away from someone else. It is often much more useful to delegate the task even though it may appear to be faster to do it yourself.

Use a mixture of Chinese and Western methods. This is a combination of first finding a way around the problem rather than through the problem. The reason for the problem may not be as obvious as you believe, or for the reasons you believe. The roadblock may be created by entirely different factors. The objective is to find a way around the roadblock and reach a mutually acceptable solution that gives you the most of what you need.

It is difficult to think about these issues from a truly Chinese perspective, so I found it useful to ask the obstructer, "What would you suggest is the best way to avoid this problem?" The answer is often very helpful and provides a good solution. When the question is asked in the right way then the correct answer is given. It may be frustrating, but it is effective. But note, do not ask this question after you have just spent the last 15 minutes arguing. Ask the question when the problem is still young and positions have not hardened.

Another approach is to use the other Chinese method. For small issues you simply proceed without asking permission. Sometimes it is easier to simply do it, and handle the consequences rather than initiate a long drawn out bureaucratic approval process.

A good example of this is airline seating. It is very difficult to book a window seat for instance. However, once you are on the plane, it is very easy to swap seats with somebody. Often you simply take a spare window seat and the person who was booked in that seat will simply move to another seat. There is a flexibility when you do not seek permission through official channels. However, this approach should be used with caution, and only in relation to smaller issues.

3. **No clear itemisation when it comes to finances. They just give a ballpark figure with no breakdown when asking us to pay for the event expenses. After much trouble, we finally got the financial items, but still no figure breakdown. This included many financial items not previously agreed to.**

## POTENTIAL REASONS

The Chinese balance sheet is complicated by several factors. The first is the difference between a *fa piao* and a receipt. A *fa piao* is an official government receipt for taxation purposes. It is an accountable form in Western terms. A receipt is specifically the equivalent of a cash register printout. It has no formal standing. When we ask for receipts people often think we mean a *fa piao* and these are simply not obtainable for many transactions.

The second is the use of cash. Many items, large and small, are paid for in cash. It's a consequence of a payment system that does not run on credit and debit cards. Often the cash is not fully recorded with an exact paper trail as we are accustomed to. Cash purchases may be in the order of 3,000 to 6,000 RMB, and made without a paper trail.

If you are using WePay then itemisation or tracking becomes easier with WePay transaction records. Shifting away from cash to digital settlement is a key objective in the anti-corruption campaigns.

Breakdowns tend to be figure or line items, rather than specific items. Remember also the background work done by the other side may include some facilitation expenditure which is not itemised. Descriptions and meanings of line item descriptions may also differ.

## POTENTIAL SOLUTIONS

Make it clear when you need or do not need a *fapiao* — official chopped government receipt — and when a *shou ju* 收据 or WeChat transaction record is acceptable. A *shou ju* is a printed receipt, the equivalent of a cash register tape in Western terms.

It is difficult, and often impossible to get itemisation for this so the focus must be on what has been delivered. If the delivery is satisfactory and it is within the ball park budget figure, then it is better just to accept it.

Provide a chart of agreed budget lines and work to acquittal against budget rather than an audit of each item. This is not a satisfactory response for Western accounting, but it's a standard approach for many Chinese companies. If there is a significant variance from agreed budget amounts, then ask for details and supporting documentation.

Accurate itemisation is an aspiration, not an objective. Work with line item budgets rather than detailed budgets, just as you would if you had sub-contracted a job to a third-party provider. Remember your accounting for the project should also focus on the line item reports rather than the detail. If detail is requested from you, then use it as a lever to have matching detail from the other participants. Establish if unusual line items are substitutes for line items using Western descriptors.

Of course, there is always the possibility you are being ripped-off, but if costs are within the expected budget parameters then the detail and itemisation of costs is less important. It is frustrating from a reporting perspective.

## 4. Inaccurate post-event reports in terms of event turn-out numbers.

These are often extremely inflated.

## POTENTIAL REASONS

This is all about face. Failure to deliver is a big issue.

## POTENTIAL SOLUTIONS

If you want accurate figures, then do your own headcount and estimates. Apply a discount factor to figures you are given. Keep an accurate record of attendance at your section of the event and use this for future planning. When participating in an event for the first time try to find others who have been before to establish a more reliable guide to attendance figures.

**5. Local exhibition contractors speak little English thus unable to liaise with international exhibitors.**

## POTENTIAL REASONS

This is not unexpected. Senior and middle management may be proficient in English, but workers engaged by the hour are highly unlikely to have English skills.

## POTENTIAL SOLUTIONS

Engage local liaison staff with good translation skills and use them only for coordination with exhibition contractors. If you can speak Chinese you can do this job, but remember it will distract you from the other work you may be required to do. The details of these logistics may be more efficiently handled by specialist staff. University students studying English are often very willing to help out for a few days for a small fee.

**6. Little consideration for exhibitors. Only allow exhibitors to move into the hall 30 minutes before the exhibition officially opens, especially on Day 1. This is definitely not enough.**

## POTENTIAL REASONS

This is bureaucracy at work. Verify that these conditions also apply to all other exhibitors. If it does, then you will have to work around it. If it does not, then you will need to work through different solutions to overcome the discrimination.

## POTENTIAL SOLUTIONS

If it applies to all exhibitors then the contractors will also be aware of this limitation. They will be accustomed to working quickly. You may decide to modify the design of your display area so it can be erected and fitted out quickly. Or create a stage display that can be erected in steps with each step being self-contained. Look at other exhibitors stands and emulate their solutions.

If this rule only applies to foreign exhibitors then work with senior management to have the rule changed. The security staff will defer to instructions from a higher authority, but they will not defer to you, or to oral reports. Where possible get the instructions and clearance permission in writing and make sure it is chopped. A signed document is useless. An email is useless. It must be the original authority document and it must be chopped.

If possible, get a handphone number from the person who is issuing the authority. If necessary, ring this person, then pass the phone to the security person who is obstructing your access. An instruction issued by a WeChat exchange is increasingly accepted so it is essential you have the necessary WeChat contacts.

Co-partner with another Chinese exhibitor so you can take your material into the exhibition area and get a head start.

7. **Security guards have policemen authority. They always chase people out of the hall in a very impolite manner and are punctilious about the closing time.**

### POTENTIAL REASONS

China loves a uniform and uniforms love exercising authority. This is not a problem limited to China. The same heavy handed approach applies in many exhibition centres. This situation is not going to change.

### POTENTIAL SOLUTIONS

Start your exhibition takedown early. Try to avoid scheduling any event that ends less than 30 minutes before the official close of the exhibition.

Work with the security people in your area during the exhibition period. This may include giving them some free promotional material, hot water for their tea etc. The objective is to give them reason to start the hurry-up process at another booth display rather than yours. It buys you a few extra minutes.

But remember, the same rules apply to all exhibitors so although it is frustrating, it is an equal inconvenience for all. Watch the experienced exhibitors and when they start packing up, follow their example.

8. **Political game-play. For the official networking dinner, the government officials asked us to leave a VIP seat for their leader though he had no intention of coming. They also brought along two low-level executives to the dinner meant for C-level executives. This is actually very disrespectful. Our local colleague says they were trying to get back at us because for our government networking dinner, the international tables were not completely filled, therefore resulting in 'loss of face'. They blamed it on us though we had already notified them that we did not need so many seats.**

## POTENTIAL REASONS

This is all about face. Face is not optional in China. It is an essential part of every event and relationship. If you cause a loss of face, then expect to suffer some consequences.

## POTENTIAL SOLUTIONS

If you are over allocated seating space at an official function, then fill the spare space with name cards or with replacement representatives: Sorry, Mr Smith was called away for a meeting, or Mr Smith is feeling unwell after the long flight, but Mr Joyce is here as his representative.' It gives face — Mr Smith is in high demand — and saves face — Mr Joyce is filling the space. In this situation, it is often just a foreign face that is important, rather than the person. The essence is to provide an acceptable excuse for non-attendance, even if the excuse appears flimsy to you. The objective is to put names and people to as many seats as have been allocated.

Where low-level executives attend a higher-level dinner, then quickly rearrange seating. It is essential that all tables in any networking dinner have name cards for all seats. This allows you to control who sits where, who gets face, who loses face. Where an important guest, Mr Chen, is known not to be turning up, then after a suitable time have the seat and name card removed, or remove the name card and elevate another person to the seat. If you know the seat will be empty, ensure the positioning is at a less important area of the table. A suitable time is after the first course is served and all guests have arrived. This means guests have had the opportunity to see that Mr Chen had been invited. The fact of invitation gives face.

9. **The constant feeling of a lamb being slaughtered and that's how we all feel when organising events in China. In fact, I felt it right after I stepped out of the plane. The constant pushing and shoving. The fittest survives. So, unless the lamb turns into a wolf, the chances of it coming out alive is almost nought. I think after our first exhibition experience we have sort of graduated into baby wolves.**

## POTENTIAL REASONS

Welcome to China. The meek are trampled on and the flexible survive.

## POTENTIAL SOLUTIONS

Learn to go around the problem, not through the problem. The direct approach is often the least useful approach. Forcing someone to back down will only earn you everlasting enmity and continuing problems during the exhibition period.

Consider the problem from the other person's perspective, particularly in terms of face. Develop a solution that gives them face and allows you to achieve an outcome consistent with your objectives. It might not be exactly the same in detail, but the result will be the same.

Repeat questions from different angles to confirm the understanding is correct. Watch how others with similar problems are working, and emulate their solutions.

You have no authority, so borrow authority and face from others. This includes correctly chopped written instructions from authority figures in Chinese.

These skilled conference organisers have many things they love about working in China. Working in China is also hugely enjoyable. It is not all negative. Here are some of the advantages, compiled by the same people who highlighted the problems considered above.

## 1. Almost anything can be solved.

Almost any logistical problem can be solved at an acceptable price. It's not difficult to find big banner printers, photocopiers, designers who will work till 12 midnight or during the weekends. This is extremely helpful when things change last minute, which they always do in China.

## 2. Perks

Being an organiser in China has its perks. The suppliers treat you to lavish meals to thank you and in hope of future business. It is disrespectful not to accept as they consider themselves hosts and more so especially when you are a foreigner. They also drive you around and frequently even arrange airport transfers. But remember, you are expected to return the favour so make sure you host a meal.

## 3. Entertainment

There is endless entertainment. China is full of cities that do not sleep. Twenty-four hour luxurious massages makes for a good de-stress activity. Good and cheap shopping and good food. It's one of the most entertaining places in Asia and at affordable prices.

## 4. Supplier responsiveness

Due to constant change, the suppliers in China are very responsive to changes. Things can be achieved on a fast turnaround and suppliers are extremely flexible. Big backdrops can be printed in a few hours, 2,000 sqm of carpet can be ordered and installed on setup day.

## 5. Good people

We did meet really warm people during our trips. Our main contractor was extremely helpful and solved many problems for us. They are very responsible people and we will recommend them in a second. Talk to other foreign exhibitors and compare notes. Develop relationships and many of the problems become smaller and easier to solve. The cheapest solution is not always the best.

## CHINA BUSINESS BITE

What you already know about your business is rarely directly transferable to a Chinese environment. Flexibility, understanding and cultural sensitivity are essential for success.

# Chapter 15

# NO CASH OR DOLLARS PLEASE

Central to business engagement with China is the advanced e-commerce environment. Something as simple as buying a freshly squeezed orange juice is completed using the ubiquitous WePay, but the back end of the process is very different from that used by ApplePay. The juice seller gets the full value of the WePay sale — no commissions or fees are deducted and that radically changes the e-commerce landscape.

This e-commerce sophistication extends to the use of a sovereign digital currency and the application of blockchain distributed ledgers to cross-border transactions and customs clearances. The WeChat universe and advanced Artificial Intelligence applications have digitalised Chinese lives in ways that Western countries struggle to comprehend because their internet structures lag behind China's 5G implementation.

It is not a level playing field. It slopes upwards from the less sophisticated to the more sophisticated and the assumption that Western methods lie at the top is flawed.

There are two consequences. The first is the need for Western business to accept the need to catch up and to develop products and services accordingly. The second consequence is a move by Western countries to isolate China or decouple. This is fatal for companies that wish to do business in China.

The Belt and Road Initiative provides an opportunity to expand the use of the Chinese sovereign digital currency outside the borders of China. Foreign companies transacting with Chinese companies for supplies, workers being paid wages and financing of projects through digital yuan loans all avoid the increased risk posed by interference in the SWIFT settlement system. This is an application of extra-territoriality.

Extra-territoriality is a discredited concept from the age of Imperialism. Extra-territoriality is making a comeback in a new form that impacts on the ability of business to do business. This has the potential for a major impact on international trade, innovation, and investment.

Extra-territoriality has now gone digital. It is enforced not with gunboats, but with digital lockouts. In 2020, the US Bureau of Industry and Security introduced regulations with extra territorial effect. At first glance the proposed law seems to impact only US companies, but closer reading identifies wider application.

The Bureau of Industry and Security amended the Export Administration Regulations to expand licence requirements on exports, re-exports, and in-country transfers of items intended for military end use or military end users in China.

The new rule broadens the definition of military end uses to include any item that 'supports or contributes' in any way to the military. These are items that have both civilian and military application. A modern military is like a large corporation and draws on just as many items for its operation, from office supplies to ordinary motor vehicles. The electronic infrastructure that keeps a corporation in operation and software that manages corporate logistics flows is no different to the requirements of a military application. Now this would be labelled as dual use because it "supports or contributes" to the operation of military items and these transactions will be off-limits to "any US resident, citizen or entity organised under the laws of the United States". These same measures were initiated against TikTok and WeChat.

The reach of US regulations beyond the statutory borders of the United States is a modern exercise in extra-territoriality. Unlike the gunboat enforcement of old, the modern enforcement method is achieved through the weaponisation of the US dollar-dominated SWIFT trade settlement system. This may involve refusing bank access to CHIPS, a New York-based clearing house through which 95% of all dollar transactions are routed. A unilateral decision taken by US regulators can strip a non-compliant company of any ability to transact international business in US dollars.

China is taking action designed to counter dollar weaponisation and so provide investors and businesses with a choice. This is the further development of a Belt and Road Initiative based trade settlement system as an alternative to dollar settlement. Essential to this is the rapid development and deployment of a sovereign digital currency within China and then followed by regional adoption.

A sovereign digital currency provides a functional alternative to the dollar settlement system and blunts the impact of any sanctions or threats of exclusion both at a country and company level. It may also facilitate integration into globally traded currency markets with a reduced risk of politically inspired disruption. These two settlement systems — US dollar and China Sovereign Digital — may operate side by side, or if need be, on a mutually exclusive basis.

Many in the West embrace the idea that "If you want peace, prepare for war". The Taoist sage Laozi suggested the alternative: "If there is to be peace in the world... There must be peace between neighbours".

China sees trade as a defensive tool and this understanding runs as a common thread through Chinese history. The West sees trade as a weapon to be wielded to force others into submission. This cultural heritage means the West most often sees trade through this historical lens, believing countries have an obligation to trade and that trade can be used as a weapon. They believe China thinks the same way.

China fully understands the way the West uses trade as a weapon. China has a century of occupation by European powers as evidence of this thinking. However, China continues to use the right to trade as a tool of diplomacy, not as a weapon of war, although Western leaders, bound by historical blinkers, often fail to see the difference.

These are broad brush strokes countered by specific short-lived counter examples. However, this broad brush remains a useful analytical tool to examine essential philosophical differences and the way

China uses trade to try to achieve peace between neighbours without the use of extra-territorial policies.

The Chinese trade system was a system of tribute built around mutual trade and the right, but not obligation, to trade. China exchanged goods with its neighbours in return for its neighbours not threatening China's borders. Hence, China was interested first and foremost in using trade as a method of ensuring security against attack by its surrounding states.

Western thinking equates tribute with a tax paid by vassal states. In the Chinese system, tribute was part of a reciprocal gift giving — a process that even today defines even the smallest of Chinese business relationships. The return gift from China was the right to trade with China. The cost of the reciprocal gift giving to the Chinese treasury was in fact economically ruinous. Some scholars argue that it was this ongoing trade deficit that effectively weakened the Ming dynasty to the extent that it was vulnerable to a successful attack from the less powerful Manchu.

The Chinese system of tribute involved giving the surrounding states the right to trade with China in exchange for a guarantee they would not attack China. The Great Wall in all its iterations was built to protect China from the Western Eurasian Steppe Xiongnu nomads and their successors who would not accept this bargain. The Great Wall in Western China defines the limits of Chinese expansion. The surrounding states were bought off with trade agreements and privileges to create a buffer against attack.

Contrast this understanding with the Western understanding of 'tribute' which comes from Medieval European politics. Here tribute is a polite name for tax, and is synonymous with vassal states. In return for protection, and a guarantee of non-aggression, the vassal state was required to pay tribute tax to the larger state.

Unfortunately, we have confused the Western Medieval relationship between tribute tax and vassal states with the Chinese practice of using the tribute mechanism to establish peaceful relations with surrounding states. This misunderstanding impacts on our understanding of the events in the South China Sea. It colours our response to China's preference for bilateral agreements rather than multilateral agreements. This explains why China prefers to deal bilaterally with the other claimants to parts of the South China Sea, rather than through a collective resolution to those disputes.

It helps explain why frustrated Westerners get the impression that their trade proposals delivered to Chinese colleagues are regarded as a 'right' rather than an obligation to do business.

The history of Chinese foreign relations can be interpreted as a persistent desire to protect the heartland by maintaining peaceful relations with its neighbours.

These broad brush strokes are as useful for understanding Chinese peace imperatives as the broad brush strokes of American exceptionalism are for understanding the evangelical imperatives of American trade and foreign policy. Historically China has used trade to secure its borders and the Belt and Road Initiative is an extension of this heritage. The West, and more recently, America, has used trade to expand its borders.

Any Western withdrawal from China trade and engagement leads to the strengthening of Belt and Road Initiative as a champion of both free trade and trade free from the bully behaviour of large nations who care little for the interests of others. The Belt and Road Initiative is alive and well, with continued momentum to establish an alternative to trade and exchange structures dominated by protectionist Western markets.

The anti-China media headlines are not above our paygrade. They have a direct impact on the way we structure investment portfolios. They impact the way we engage in business with China and use China as a source of materials or services in supply chains and business delivery. The headlines of manoeuvres in the South China Sea and sanctions are attempts to contain China but these bully actions are also designed to throttle China. There is not much we can do about this, but we cannot ignore the impact, not just on investment portfolios, but on business activity and development. Central to this is an improved understanding of what is involved in the Belt and Road Initiative because this is the new foundation of China trade.

Belt and Road cannot be ignored or misunderstood because it will change the way your business pays and gets paid in China.

## CHINA BUSINESS BITE

The weaponisation of the SWIFT dollar settlement system changes the way cross-border business is transacted. Businesses need to prepare for this change and for participation in a sophisticated digital e-commerce economy under the Belt and Road Initiative umbrella.

# Chapter 16

# MAPPING THE SILK ROAD

The string of camels plodded their way across the desert sands, snorting in derision at their inexperienced tourist riders. The blue sky stretched towards endless horizons, the mirage teasing out shapeless illusions of water. It was, and was not, a typical Central Australian desert scene. These were twin humped Bactrian camels moping towards the Crescent Lake oasis in the remote Gansu province of Western China, near the border of Inner Mongolia.

I was in Gansu to speak at a Belt and Road Initiative (BRI) round-table conference and to explore areas of co-operation for Northern Territory businesses. It was a suitable location, as Dunhuang is located at one of the major crossroads in the ancient Silk Road. I invited Gansu officials to consider bringing a delegation to Central Australia to meet with government agencies and indigenous organisations to explore these areas of co-operation.

These areas of exchange include the management of tourism impacts on fragile environments and the environmental monitoring of remote locations, including mining and feral animal impacts. Like Central Australia, Gansu is concerned with the management and preservation of cultural relics and sites in an arid environment. For hundreds of years Dunhuang in Gansu province offered protection for the Diamond Sutra in the Mogao caves and to thousands of other ancient scrolls.

Just how all this relates to the Belt and Road Initiative illustrates why a better understanding of the initiative is critical for business success in China. We are not talking about sourcing cheap consumer components or selling consumer services into China. The BRI impact is on investment, capital flows, and high-end communications, 5G and Artificial Intelligence economies. The BRI impact is on trade flows, cross-border transactions and trade protocols. Nested in this policy framework are myriad opportunities that go beyond the simplistic idea that the BRI is only about physical infrastructure and somehow a security threat.

The Belt and Road Initiative is now integral to all investment and business decisions made by Chinese companies, corporates and SOEs so we need to understand both the situation that prompted this policy and how it has subsequently developed. The chances of success are improved when business and investment proposals are framed within this context.

Getting involved with China's Belt and Road Initiative (BRI) is described by some politicians and media as 'ill advised' because it is all about China's "growing territorial ambitions" with its focus on infrastructure. This characterisation is both ill-informed and the Western obsession with the infrastructure component is inaccurate, so it is worth taking the time to refresh our understanding of the BRI.

The poor level of analysis is also demonstrated by confusion about how the 'Road' component relates to sea lanes. Every mariner knows the 'roads' are deep-water safe harbours where ships wait to unload cargo.

The BRI represents the transformation of China from a regional into a global power. Many argue that China is not setting out to destroy the Western-led world order, although this is the view often adopted by the US and some of its allies. The initiatives in the areas of finance, currency, trade, and security are meant to provide China with alternatives and so reduce its dependency on the current order without reducing its support for the current order. However, it remains clear that China wants to see the international order adjusted in a way that allows it to have a degree of influence that reflects its economic position. The BRI is part of this process.

This is not a repeat of the Cold War with the Soviet Union because even at its height, the Soviet Union could not lay claim to any significant economic clout. It was a military state that struggled to feed its own people. China is a global economic power and its attention is primarily focused on trade relationships as a way of alleviating poverty and moving towards a moderately prosperous society. These may sound like the familiar lip-service aspirations of Western politicians, but China is absolutely serious about them as shown already by its remarkable achievements in lifting millions out of poverty.

The foundation of the Belt and Road policies lie in the post-2008 collapse of global markets. The question faced by Chinese authorities was 'What should we do with China's Foreign Reserves?' because they were no longer considered a low risk option. The risk quotient was heightened under President Trump and his anti-China advisors.

The solution was to redirect foreign reserves away from investment in US bonds and towards a broader platform of China-friendly investment. This required a long-term reassessment of China's role in the global financial system and the inevitable internationalisation of the yuan. Most obviously, the redirection is observed in the development of the Asian Infrastructure Investment Bank and Silk Road Fund.

These objectives have been given additional impetus by the increasing weaponisation of the US dollar SWIFT settlement system as discussed in the previous chapter.

Implementation was also broadened to embrace four major pillars of the Belt and Road. These pillars have been subsequently refined as the policy morphed from New Silk Road/Maritime Silk Road to One Belt One Road and then to the current Belt and Road Initiative. At its core, the BRI policy is a global market concept. It is not a treaty, nor a trade agreement. It is a standard of agreed trade protocols and processes for cross-border transactions.

The BRI is meant to provide China with market alternatives without reducing its support for the current order.

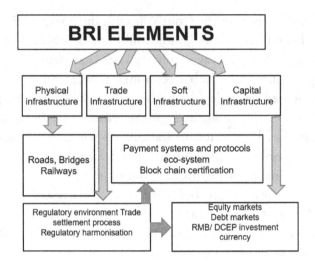

There are four dimensions of BRI, and they change to structure of trade and cross-border transactions. The dimensions are:

- Physical infrastructure as this facilitates the growth of trade. High-speed rail connections are a key component because they open up new areas in Asia and Central Asia. Better roads and bridges are also essential to trade development. This physical infrastructure also includes ports.

Western commentary has a strong focus on this infrastructure build because it suspects it has a military purpose and thus class this as a threat.

- Trade infrastructure is perhaps more important than roads and bridges. This includes the removal of trade barriers and standardisation of trade regulation. Trade settlement processes are an essential enabler of trade. China is leading the way in many areas, such as blockchain customs clearances. Despite this, China supports the WTO as the primary mechanism for resolving trade disputes.
- Soft infrastructure is essential because it deals with payment systems and protocols. This is an essential eco-system that includes a broader

application of blockchain certification not just for payments, but also in fighting product substitution.

Countries within the BRI will participate in a harmonised set of trade and trade settlement standards that will make cross-border trade more efficient.

- The final component is capital infrastructure. Currency integration is a precursor to the growth of China's capital markets. Further opening of the capital account, debt markets and the liberalisation of investment conditions are part of this process. More recently this has included the application of a China Digital Currency which prevents trade being held hostage to the US dominated SWIFT currency transfer system.

At its core the BRI has the concepts of shared prosperity that recognises and accepts the diversity of political structures. These concepts sound insincere to Western ears, accustomed as they are to the Machiavellian idea that all foreign relations are about power, conquest and submission.

This is now the framework for all business activity in China. For some it will be not much more than lip-service, but for others it lies at the core of business and investment decisions. Framing your business in this BRI context provides a competitive advantage.

Some observers have significant concerns about aspects of BRI, but this often rests on a one-dimensional view most often projected by military and security agencies. More informed engagement with the BRI is essential.

The first step is to acknowledge the legitimacy of the BRI policy. This is a major policy initiative. China is the world's second largest economy and like large economies before it, China feels the need to engage the global community across wider dimensions than it has in the past.

Governments need to establish mechanisms to understand the BRI, to monitor its development and its progress. Western countries understand US policy in fine detail and considerable multi-agency resources are directed towards this end. The same level of engagement should be applied to understanding the BRI so governments can respond in a more informed manner to policy developments.

Engagement includes regular international forums to discuss BRI, to evaluate its progress, to raise concerns and to identify areas of co-operation. This could be made a formal part of the existing leadership dialogues with China's inclusion in an expanded G7 or G8.

The BRI is a significant and developing complex of policies and it requires an adjustment of thinking around foreign and trade policy. It makes for a poor policy environment when the BRI is viewed mainly through a security and military lens where it has been worked into a narrative about China and the South China Sea, and unease about China's global ambitions.

As overseas BRI investment develops, it is increasingly dictating not only the terms of financing but is also altering the global competitive landscape by defining and exporting technical standards for everything from artificial intelligence to hydropower.

So, this has mainly impacted domestically as the Chinese Government develops its own set of standards for companies operating within its borders. Western companies outside of China have largely ignored these developments.

Chinese regulators are now starting to translate those standards into English and the other languages used by countries on the Silk Road. This is a clear sign that these BRI standards are meant to be exported overseas.

The ability of Western governments to set international standards has benefited their economies. These standards serve as 'soft infrastructure' bridges between developing innovations and the commercialisation of those innovations. A universally accepted USB plug design is just as vital to modern commerce as a new bridge.

This is where the BRI will have a lasting impact. The return on investment for a bridge is less important in the long term than the adoption of Chinese standards on everything from construction to finance, from cross-border e-commerce transaction to data management.

When China builds high-speed rail links it also exports key technical standards for this type of construction. Countries tend to voluntarily adopt these standards and it becomes soft infrastructure. China's revisions to its National Standardisation Law and Cyber Security Law have international implications.

Can your company submit engineering and design proposals that are compatible with BRI standards? Can your company implement quality control that is compliant with BRI protocols? Does your innovative AI solution integrate with BRI connectivity? These are key questions to answer if you are doing business with China.

The broad and widespread impact of BRI policies on cross-border trade, e-commerce, operational systems, regulatory structures, and trade relationships demand that countries create a role for themselves within BRI discussions. At times business organisations like the Silk Road Chambers of International Commerce and others will be required to lead the way for politicians to provide a platform that enables each country to lift its China relationship to a more sophisticated level.

This is the key choice for some countries. They can continue to mischaracterise the BRI or they can develop an informed understanding and discussion to engage with the real BRI and as businesspeople we have an obligation to provide better information for use in making policy decisions.

Business must recognise that these soft infrastructure developments do not directly challenge the ability of Western companies to innovate. But they do challenge their ability to commercialise innovation and market into those countries which have adopted the Chinese soft infrastructure framework. This is why engagement with the Belt and Road Initiatives is so essential.

## CHINA BUSINESS BITE

The Belt and Road Initiative offers multiple, new opportunities in a different business environment. Proposals consistent with the BRI enjoy faster approvals.

# Chapter 17

# TAPPING SILK ROAD OPPORTUNITIES

In the Belt and Road pavilion in Shenzhen, the lanolin-based skin care products were quickly disappearing off the shelves. Rich soft white woollen fleeces were in hot demand. Bottles of very very expensive honey sat ready for collection alongside bottles of red wine. The inevitable mountain of infant milk powder was quickly reduced to a hummock. All boasted of their clean, green and pollution-free pedigree.

However, none of this came from Australia which prides itself on being the supplier of choice for all these products. Of course, France also prides itself on its wine, New Zealand for its honey, the Netherlands for its infant milk powder and several central Asian countries for their woollen fleeces. They all tell their domestic farmers and industry that their country is the supplier of choice to China.

These products all came from countries scattered along the Silk Road. There was an Australian pavilion although Australia is not formally part of the Belt and Road community. Australian products are not unique and nor are they necessarily preferred over other similar products. Like all countries doing business with China, they sit in a very competitive environment where ease of market access is one of the competitive advantages. Increasingly, that ease of access is being provided by the Belt and Road.

The Belt and Road policy is a global market concept. It is not a treaty, or a trade agreement, but it is becoming a collection of agreed trade protocols and processes for cross-border transactions.

Exporters know that the trade and border regulations in Indonesia, for instance, are very different to those in the United States, the EU, or

Japan. Formal Free Trade agreements do not necessarily filter down to a common set of regulatory procedures at the customs gate. An important aspect of the BRI process is working from the bottom up to smooth out and standardise these regulatory procedures. It works to eliminate what are often called 'behind the border barriers' that often frustrate the practical implementation of high-level strategic trade agreements. These barriers determine the way exports of live fish, chilled beef, fresh mangoes and seafood are processed when they land in China.

The Belt and Road Initiative is not a trade agreement, nor a formalised treaty. Participation is by way of a Memorandum of Understanding. New Zealand, for instance, has signed a comprehensive MOU which enables it to more easily integrate existing trade agreements within the BRI framework. One result is that New Zealand Manuka honey is selling at US$328 for a 500 gram bottle while the equivalent Australian honey has barely touched the market.

For political reasons, some Western countries have decided not to be directly involved in the BRI, although they are willing to work with third parties who are involved with the BRI. These countries remain on the edges of this emerging economic bloc.

This is politics and as much as SMEs would like to argue that they are not involved in politics, the reality is that politics does impact on what business we can do and how it is done. Your business success in China may require you to politely distance yourself from national policy. There are a number of approaches that are available in dealing with this BRI policy.

The first step is to acknowledge the legitimacy of the Belt and Road policy. This is a major policy initiative within the region and potentially beyond the region. China is the world's second largest economy and like large economies before it, China feels the need to engage the global community across wider dimensions than it has in the past.

The first step leads to the second step — engagement. For business this means involvement in BRI projects, business opportunities and investment attraction. Engagement requires a better understanding of how the BRI fits into Chinese investment decisions as explained in the previous chapter. Engagement for governments has a different meaning.

Governments need to establish mechanisms to understand the BRI, to monitor its development and its progress. Western countries understand United States policy in fine detail and considerable multi-agency resources are directed towards this end. They need to apply the same level of engagement with this Chinese policy so their governments can respond effectively to policy developments.

Engagement starts from a regular forum to discuss the BRI, to evaluate its progress, to raise concerns and to identify areas of co-operation. This could be incorporated as a specific dialogue, or made a formal part of the existing leadership dialogues.

At a business level, this includes the involvement of business councils in multi-lateral organisations like the Silk Road Chambers of International Commerce which brings together business chambers to develop improved understanding of the BRI.

The third step is adjustment. Currently the BRI is most frequently viewed through a security and military lens. It has been worked into a narrative about China and the South China Sea, and generates a general feeling of unease about China's global ambitions.

As discussed in previous chapters, the BRI is a significant complex of policies and it does require an adjustment of thinking around foreign and trade policy.

The fourth step is to draw red lines. This step should follow the first three steps, but a lot of current focus is on the red-line rhetoric, be it with regard to the South China Sea, the development of 5G, or the potential for cyber-attacks. This reflects a one-dimensional understanding of the BRI and can lead to the inappropriate placement of red lines.

Countries need to be alert for potential misuse of the BRI initiatives to advance agendas that do not serve their interests. They need to make clear their concerns.

This is most effectively achieved through an acknowledgement of the BRI policies and engagement with BRI policies so that the understanding is more sophisticated and informed.

The fifth step is to carve out a role within the BRI. This is at the core of the philosophical argument. Some believe that the BRI should be opposed and China's ambitions curtailed or contained so that the existing status quo is not disrupted. If this is your belief then your business in China is unlikely to succeed.

The alternative view is that China's ambitions should be understood and managed. The broad and widespread impact of BRI policies on cross-border trade, e-commerce, operational systems, regulatory structures and trade relationships demand that countries create a role for themselves within BRI discussions. Adopt this path and your business dramatically improves its chances of success.

The sixth step is the logical cumulation of the first five steps. This is to positively integrate the BRI into the overall framework of China relations. The BRI provides a platform that enables a country to deepen its relationships with China and lift it to a more sophisticated level.

This is the key choice for countries in the region. We can continue to look at, and mischaracterise, the BRI from the outside, or we can discuss the BRI from within.

There are advantages for every business in becoming familiar with, and involved with the policy structures that are part of the BRI framework as this provides opportunities for businesses and encourages Chinese investment. Our objective is to get more of our products or services into China.

## CHINA BUSINESS BITE

The Belt and Road Initiative is the foundation policy for business and cross-border trade in China. Ignorance of the policy, or refusal to become involved, limits your ability to do business in China and with other countries involved in the BRI.

# Chapter 18

# TENDRILS OF THE SILK ROAD

Skimming the mountain tops and weaving through the clouds gives truth to the literal translation of Yunnan — south of the clouds — and a new insight into China's Silk Road. A 200-kilometre journey that would have taken a full day or more just a few years ago can now be completed in a little over two hours. It would be made on a four-lane expressway that carves its way through the jungle and the mountains. Tunnels are often two to three kilometres long and the road a series of gentle gradients and sedate curves. Occasionally, one gets a glimpse of the old road, with switchback curves, steep descents, and even steeper ascents.

Running alongside the expressway is the high-speed railway that will soon link Kunming with Bangkok via Laos. This is typical of the logistics framework that allows the most remote corners of China to reach new markets and which also allows your products and services to efficiently reach these remote provinces.

This is the new China opened to new markets by policies of poverty alleviation. These changes increase disposable income and encourage new aspirations. These are markets beyond the east coast mega-cities.

The result is an explosion of agriculture. This part of Yunnan appears to be the fruit bowl of China. In addition, the hills are knitted with neatly serried rows of rubber trees. The expressway has given unprecedented market access. The railway will boost that even further.

In the China-Laos border town of Mohan, I stood on the edge of a huge hardstand foundation of the marshalling yards, and the passenger platform that will become the central border clearing station for the railway as it crosses into Laos. It's a US$500 million project that will be completed on time and at a high-quality standard.

The physical infrastructure is essential, but without a suitable metaphysical infrastructure the full potential of the railway cannot be met. Blockchain technology is an essential part of this metaphysical infrastructure. It will provide certified digital clearance for cargoes, reducing the cross-border transit times to a bare minimum. Kunming to Bangkok is estimated to be 8 hours.

The road expressway has transformed the economic activity of southwestern Yunnan. It allows existing agriculture businesses to expand because markets can be reached more quickly. It encourages the development of new industries that were inconceivable in the past because of logistic and transport constraints.

The extension of the high-speed rail network into Laos and Thailand will have a similar transformative impact on economic activity. Although there is a natural tendency to focus on the short-term business benefits of the infrastructure build involved with the railway, this focus misses the larger economic development picture. It also misses the transformative nature of the Belt and Road Initiatives. This is a generation changing policy structure. It changes the nature of the trade relationships and the structure of the trade relationships in the region.

It is essential that businesses understand these longer-term implications so they can position themselves to be fully involved in this emerging economic structure. The Belt and Road is moving much faster than many outside of China realise.

Around the same time as the old Silk Road came into existence as a trade route, the Tea Horse Tea Road in Southwestern China was also thriving. This steep and narrow pathway wound its way through the jungle and over the cloud covered hills of Yunnan to transport tea by horse and donkey to the tables of emperors and other nobles in capitals as diverse as Xi'an, Nanjing and Beijing. It was a tendril of the Silk Road.

These tendrils still exist as I was reminded as I puffed my way up narrow mountains trails in Zhu Lin village near the Myanmar border in Southwestern Yunnan to look at tea trees between 600 and 700 years old. These are the long leaf Yunnan tea trees, planted not in the neat serried rows seen in the tea plantations near Hangzhou Xi Hu mountains, but in oddly spaced plantings clinging to impossibly steep hillsides.

Leaves from the older trees command up to 15,000 Renminbi a kilo. The average price is around 5,000 Renminbi a kilo. Buyers come to collect the leaves from specific trees to produce the best of Yunnan's renowned Pu'er tea.

But the tea no longer departs by the treacherous Tea Horse Tea trails. It is connected to the broader New Silk Road which enables buyers to more easily access these remote tea growing areas. It allows special ancient trees to be individually harvested rather than having their leaves lumped together with younger trees and then sold for a lower price. This treasured ancient tree growth has massively boosted the incomes of farmers who just a few years ago were classed as impoverished tea growers.

To the south of Zhu Lin, the gaping maw of the new railway tunnel sits on the opposite bank of the Lan Cang Jiang — Mekong river — near Daizuyuan village. In a coffer dam, the pylons for the railway bridge spanning the river are under construction, ready to carry the high-speed railway across the river and onwards to Kunming. Nearby are the giant towers that will carry the suspension road bridge across the Mekong.

This is the Belt and Road Initiative in infrastructure action as we expect to see it, but this is not the complete story of the Silk Road.

Earlier, in a Dai minority village, I watched traditional weaving on hand looms. The beautiful silken prayer shawls are created from the weft and warp of delicate tendrils of silken thread. The New Silk Road has the same construction. Beyond the large-scale infrastructure projects are the little projects, the local projects, the small-scale projects that lift people from poverty by enabling more efficient trade through improved logistics.

The 600-year-old Pu'er tea tree has seen generations of change but perhaps no change as significant as now. No matter whether you are buying, transporting, or drinking tea, the impact of the Belt and Road Initiative is felt as it is across all business activity in the region.

This growth in economic activity offers opportunities for SME businesses to assist with many projects so it is essential that we become involved in the Belt and Road Initiative development.

## CHINA BUSINESS BITE

Moving beyond the east coast cities was difficult but that has changed as Belt and Road Initiative projects make remote and developing China more accessible. These are new opportunities if your business is compatible with BRI.

# Chapter 19

# BRI CO-OPERATION

Engage, Exclude or Enrage? The 3E's summarise policy approaches to China. Some Western countries add a dangerous fourth E to the list — Entitlement — and this impacts on companies that have been foreign investment portfolio favourites.

This has everything to do with the way SMEs are able to access China markets. They do not have the power of the business giants so SMEs use the influence of their business councils to engage in the policy debate.

Exclude is an apt description of the political pressure currently being applied to hinder competition. This includes insinuations that superior Chinese development in fields as diverse as AI, 5G, the internet of things and solar technology is a result of IP theft, and that this poses an ill-defined security threat. Many business leaders regard the concerted attack on Huawei, TikTok and WeChat as motivated primarily by commercial, not security, considerations.

Enraging China is an inevitable result of the demand that China change its industrial and economic model — and change it in a way that is disadvantageous to China. This includes demands that China restructure its economy to stop the activities of State-Owned Enterprises on the false assumption that this is the Chinese business model. In fact, more than 90% of Chinese business is privately owned.

These demands trigger memories of the century of humiliation where China did give-in to demands from foreign countries. To accede to these modern-era demands would mean that the millions who aspire to middle class status in China would not be able to achieve it.

Some Western businesses in Asia have developed a growing sense of entitlement in their approach to China export markets. Entitlement means that they think that China is obligated to import corn, or beef, social media or milk, no matter what quality they choose to send and no matter if the service is illegal in China.

Engagement with China means more open and less confrontational discussion. It includes participation in policy forums and developing intellectual exchanges that go beyond simply selling education to undergraduates. This creates a better and more nuanced understanding of the policy environment and encourages the development of more sophisticated policy responses to China. This in turn means that businesses can engage with Chinese businesses in a more stable and effective manner. This provides better opportunities for SMEs working in China.

Singapore has pursued an effective engagement strategy with China. Some other countries in the region have been less successful. These sovereign policy approaches need to be factored into investment portfolio and business decisions.

Engagement doesn't mean agreement with everything that China does. Engagement means that acknowledgement that more is achieved through open, considered and ongoing dialogue.

Engagement delivers a fifth E and that is a competitive Edge. It brings an edge not just to government to government relationships, but to business to business connections. These are approaches investors need to consider when constructing investment portfolios designed for exposure to China business. This edge creates a better environment for SME business.

All of this is difficult for an individual business to achieve, although it is this environment that makes business easy or difficult. Membership of business councils allows them to show how China's Belt and Road policy is compatible with national development policies. They have the representative power to encourage governments and businesses to engage with the BRI policy. They must overcome the barriers to understanding and this includes working with business organisations like the Silk Road Chamber of International Commerce which bring together business leaders.

This has become even more important since President Trump has increased his destruction of the global trading environment. This is a serious economic challenge but fortunately the Belt and Road Initiative provides an alternative structure that supports the WTO and other cross-border trade processes. The first task as business organisations is to help members and governments to understand the foundation of the BRI, so they can counter-balance the anti-trade narrative that is coming from the United States and which is distorting good policymaking in other economies.

The second task is to accurately recognise the barriers that are being created and work towards overturning these barriers by promoting policy discussion with business and government leaders.

As discussed in previous chapters, the Belt and Road is a far more sophisticated policy framework than just roads, bridges and transport corridors. It is essential that we understand the trade infrastructure, and the soft infrastructure aspects of Belt and Road. This includes the development of the regulatory environment with regulatory harmonisation, supporting WTO processes and advancing trade settlement processes. It includes payment systems, standards and protocols in everything from 5G to blockchain certification.

There are three barriers that business chambers must recognise and attempt to overcome. The barriers are:

1) Tariffs and trade barriers. This includes the unilateral imposition of tariffs by the United States. It includes the US-led destruction of the global rules-based order by ignoring or undermining the operation of the World Trade Organisation. It also includes the use of third-party penalties, such as when the US threatens actions against other countries for doing business that is inconsistent with US policy.

   Business organisations must convey the concerns of their members and develop political solutions.

2) The false use of security concerns as a method of destroying business competition. These are attacks by government on business and they are designed to protect domestic business. There is a trend towards using unexplained security concerns to frustrate investment and

business. Chambers should not be afraid to use the financial media to highlight their members' concerns about these bully tactics.

3) Processes and regulations that frustrate the smooth operation of cross-border trade. Members of business organisations must be encouraged to report the new regulations and the new paperwork delays, so Chambers can present these in a coherent manner to policymakers. Chambers are the collective voice of their members.

The task of business organisations is to help their members overcome problems created by these barriers. But they also have another important task. They must educate their members and governments about the Belt and Road Initiative.

Business organisations must play their part in Belt and Road international co-operation. They articulate the concerns of their members so the operation of the Belt and Road can become more efficient. They also encourage governments and businesses to engage with and understand the BRI policy.

## CHINA BUSINESS BITE

Small businesses operate under the umbrella of national policies. Business councils provide a collective voice to raise concerns about policy direction. Your support and involvement may confer advantages for your China business.

# Chapter 20

# CHINESE MOMENTS

In popular mythology the Chinese may appear inscrutable but this is a reflection of our own lack of understanding and inability to move beyond surface impressions. Business is about people and this does not just refer to customers. People include staff, friends, clients, customers and associates. When these people are Chinese there are new dimensions added and new challenges. If you are not up to the challenge then it can become endlessly frustrating for you. Resolve these challenges and not only will your China business run more smoothly, but also enrich your experience.

Some of this frustration is sometimes called a Chinese Moment. It happens to anyone who has worked in China, or who works with the Chinese. It's a short period of intense frustration, usually over a simple problem that suddenly snowballs into confusion and misunderstanding. It's a 'pull-your-hair-out' experience that unless handled carefully, can lead to long lasting damage in a business relationship. The same also applies in reverse, and Chinese friends speak of English Moments when something that is clear and obvious to them is simply not comprehended by English speakers.

Chinese Moments cannot be avoided, but they can be minimised. They occur because the two ways of thinking are so different. We can try to understand, but it is impossible to understand completely or consistently. Our best understanding is tripped up on language that cannot be translated accurately for meaning. Many English thoughts have no adequate direct translation into Chinese. Likewise, many Chinese processes have no direct or adequate translation into English.

It's often a field of approximation, and at times when precision is required, this inadequate approximation leads directly to a Chinese Moment.

The Chinese Moment starts when each side attaches a different meaning to the same words, or concept. It's a constant challenge in working with written translations where translation is for meaning as well as literal accuracy.

Patience is required, but patience is not a solution. An answer to a question, although correct, may not resolve the issue because the question is based on an incorrect understanding. The first step is to work out what the question is really about, or more exactly, what has triggered the question. Often the confusion arises because each party is using the same words or phrases, but attaching a different meaning to them. Careful alternative questions, or rephrasing of questions about the same issue will help expose these differences.

Once you establish this, then it becomes a different task to explain the differences in understanding. The translator is often proud of their skill and reluctant to acknowledge that their understanding of the meaning may be not the same as that of an English speaker. The challenge is for you to rephrase the comment, the request, the sentence or the instruction in a way that makes sense to the listeners' understanding. I look on this as an opportunity to stretch my mental agility, but that does not mean I am able to avoid all the Chinese Moments.

In a recent column for the Shanghai Security News I wrote "this event may develop over several more days." Such a simple beginning for a Chinese Moment. "How many days is several days?" I was asked by the translator. Several is more than a couple of days but less than a week so several days would be between 3 to 5 days I replied. "So, you mean 6 days?" was the reply.

It took some discussion to establish how 6 days was derived from 'several' days. The reasoning was that several days is 3 to 5 days. I had written 'several more days' so the meaning was that the elapsed time would be 'more' than 'several'. More than 5 days plus at least one day is 6 days so this was the answer. The logic may not be impeccable but given the stress on the word 'more' the logic is unassailable.

The full Chinese Moment was avoided by a simple rewrite to "the event may develop in the next 3 to 5 days".

So where does the responsibility for understanding lie? Do we always have to give in? The answer is largely yes. When we choose to work in China it shifts the responsibility for understanding to our shoulders. When we invite Chinese business or investors to work with us in our home country, then again, we accept the responsibility and challenges of understanding. You can rest assured the Chinese side also takes these responsibilities seriously and they also try to understand the nuances of Australian, American or European behaviour and language. They find English Moments just as frustrating.

With goodwill on both sides, things proceed smoothly most of the time. It's easy to get lulled into a sense of achievement and then a Chinese Moment will develop out of something innocuous. It's a reminder of the complexity of business and relationships that are an inevitable part of working in a Chinese environment.

Chinese habits also lead to Chinese moments. It remains disconcerting to be in a meeting with senior Chinese partners when one of their smartphones rings. The current conversation stops and the Chinese partner will answer the phone and often have quite a long conversation. From a Western perspective this is quite rude behaviour, particularly in the middle of an important meeting. This is not meant to be disrespectful. It's simply a Chinese habit and it is not considered rude. It may also be a matter of face and that is a more important consideration.

In the West we value contactability. Smart phone advertising tells us we can work from anywhere and at any time because we can be contacted globally. The downside is that we can be contacted by anybody at any time. We ignore calls in meetings because its odds-on the call is not so important.

In China, lack of contactability at senior levels provides face. As mentioned in the earlier section of this book, personal contact numbers are not freely exchanged. Like their Western counterparts, many senior Chinese managers do not give out name cards, or if they do, the cards do not contain direct contact details. Business cards are routinely exchanged amongst mid-level managers, but are not compulsorily exchanged at a senior level. You may offer your name card, and not receive one in return. If you are offered a name card by a junior person, you do not have to give your name card in return. Senior managers wish to be contactable only by people from an appropriate equivalent level. It is not uncommon for business cards not to be exchanged in a meeting. This behaviour increases the further north you go in China.

So, when a senior manager's phone rings, he knows it is usually from a person of at least equivalent ranking. It would be rude for him not to take it. And by taking it, he may also assume you understand he is taking a call from somebody important. Taking the call gives him face.

You can also give yourself face by taking important calls on your smart phone in meetings. The more senior you are, the more likely it is to be assumed your caller is a person of seniority. However, remember there is a high probability someone in the room will understand your conversation, so be careful about what you discuss.

The same does not apply to WeChat conversations which, like WeChat itself, are ubiquitous. The Chinese side of the meeting makes no pretence of not answering their WeChat messages during the meeting, and the Western side hides their activity below the desktop level. These WeChat messages give delegation members a new way to communicate private observations during the meeting rather than using written notes passed by hand down the table, or whispered conversations.

Chinese Moments do not always result in frustration. They also arise when the reaction we get is not the reaction we expect. Motivating Chinese staff and capturing commitment takes different paths to those used in Western businesses.

Are you good at your work? If someone complimented you on your work, how would you respond? If you are given a task, will you say you can meet the targets?

The Western answers slip easily from our mouths. "Yes, I am good at my work. Thank you for the compliment and yes, I will meet the targets."

These are appropriate responses in a Western environment but you are less likely to hear them in a Chinese environment. This can make working on projects and schedules frustrating because we do not hear the responses we expect. Just as importantly, when we give these responses in a Chinese situation they can be misinterpreted.

We do not want to suggest one set of responses is correct and the other set is wrong. It is useful to understand how these responses can be misunderstood and lead to confusion.

Are you good at your work? The usual Chinese response is along the lines "I still have much to improve on. I am still learning." Alternatively, you might say "No, my skill is not as good as yours." This type of response does not trip easily off Western tongues, but it is part of the modesty which governs Chinese social behaviour. To say more is the equivalent of rude bragging. Latitude is given to Westerners but it is always good not to have to make use of it.

There is a reverse impact. When you hear this modest answer from others it is unwise to conclude the person lacks confidence or skill. People who are experts in their field or highly skilled will often answer in a way that downplays their skill and knowledge. It is not a subterfuge or a stratagem. It's a nod to Chinese politeness.

The same modesty applies when being given or accepting a compliment. I was with a friend and we were meeting another friend. My friend was complimented on her clothes. Instead of saying "Thank you" she replied, "No, I don't look nearly as young and pretty as you do". It is a way to return a compliment to a friend.

In similar fashion years ago, I was introduced as an 'expert' to a small group of Chinese people. It was not appropriate to return a similar compliment, particularly as I did not know them well. My response was "Na li, na li." It literally means "Where, where" but it is understood as "No, not really". The response acknowledges the compliment and accepts it without directly saying 'Thank you".

However, this "Na li, na li" response is now mainly confined to outdated textbooks and is rarely heard in the real world. It is now more often acknowledged by a polite dip of the head.

You may decide you are more comfortable with Western responses. However, it is useful to remember the seemingly indifferent response from Chinese staff to your compliments or praise is in fact a quiet acceptance and acknowledgement.

Westerners always say they can meet their target, or tell you targets cannot be met unless there are some changes made. It is direct dealing and everybody knows where they stand so it is frustrating to hear "I will do my best" or "It should be OK". These answers in the workplace reflect two things. The first is an extension of the modesty discussed above. The second is related to keeping face. If I say I will achieve something and then fail to achieve it then I will lose face. Better to say I will do my best.

To Western ears, "I will do my best" indicates a lack of confidence, an unwillingness to meet targets, or someone laying the groundwork for a later excuse for failure. For the Chinese this is a statement of intention. This Chinese response has two important consequences for Western listeners.

First, when we hear it, we should take it as a 'Yes'. People will do their best to achieve the objective and pushing them further will not often get to a 'Yes'. If the person truly cannot do the job, then you are more likely to be told it is "inconvenient".

Second, the Western response of a resounding "Yes, we can meet these targets" has a different meaning to Chinese ears. It is closer to the equivalent of a promise rather than a statement of intention. When you give a promise the consequences of failure are much more severe than just failing to reach a target. A promise is considered much more binding in its intent. In China I always agree to 'Do my best' unless it is impossible — sorry, inconvenient.

Modesty and humility are important features of relationships in China. They should not be mistaken for weakness or lack of confidence or commitment.

First impressions in China always include a new awareness of the meaning of crowds and the disorientation of hearing and reading a totally foreign language. It's the crowds and behaviour in crowds that many people find most challenging and which brings on their first Chinese Moment.

Standing in a crowded queue at the airport, someone stepped heavily on my foot. It is an inevitable part of being involved in a large crowd — *ren shan ren hai* 人山人海. Literally, 'people mountain, people sea'. My first reaction was to expect an apology. Instead I was met with a rather sharp admonishment, which loosely translates into "Why is your foot under my foot?"

This is not rudeness, although to Western ears it is. It is the result of a different concept of personal space. We are accustomed to leaving about one body width in space between ourselves and others. This degree of space is a luxury and too large in China. Leave this much space in a queue and people will cut into the queue in front of you. When it is suggested they should go to the back of the line, they ask "Why did you leave so much space. I thought you weren't part of the queue".

When you are supermarket shopping, there is no apparent order in the queues. You stand in a nominal queue. People shuffle into the line, bit by bit, and unless you are careful, there is suddenly another person in front of you in an already incredibly long line.

Grey haired old ladies are the worst, nudging into you with their shopping trolleys. The first time this happened, I did the Western thing and gave way. Trouble was, she was part of a train of shopping trolleys. Three others were attached to her shopping trolley. Just friends. Quite different shoppers, but a group of grannies intent on busting into any space available. Thereafter I jealously guarded my position in the line.

Chinese moments are frustrating but they are also a reminder that as foreigners in China, we have much to learn before we are fully comfortable and competent in this environment.

## CHINA BUSINESS BITE

The same words mean different things to different ears. Similar situations lead to disparate behaviours. Chinese Moments are inevitable, but do your best to avoid them by understanding their origins.

# Chapter 21

# PHRASES OF FRUSTRATION

A simple question asked of a Beijing waitress delivers an unexpected result. "Do you know where the toilet is?" a Western friend asked. She looked at him with disdain. "Of course I do," she said and walked off to another table, leaving him wondering how to locate the toilet. Asking "How long before we arrive?" can generate a strange response. "It's another 5 kilometres" rather than "Another ten minutes". Rephrase the question to "How much time before we arrive?" and you get your desired answer. We chuckle at these misunderstandings but in a business meeting the consequences may be more significant.

Language is a tricky beast. It allows us to say exactly what we want to say, or if our ability in a second language is not so good, then it prevents us from conveying the shades of meaning we intend. As listeners we have an obligation to listen more carefully. As speakers we have an obligation to think more clearly before we speak. Survival is the difference between translation and the unique features of language habit. These nuances are mildly amusing in private conversation, but they become critical in a business environment.

Language has many traps. Unless we are very fluent in Chinese, most of us will avoid using Chinese except in situations where meaning is not absolutely critical. However, there is always a temptation to use your smattering of Chinese for simple phrases and expressions. This sounds like it should be a safe area, but it conceals some hidden dangers. It works both ways, and Chinese friends may also use small safe English phrases which don't quite convey their intended meaning.

I work with a Chinese colleague who has very good command of English, but he had a habit of frequently saying "I know" during conversations. In terms of English usage, we understand that this means you already know what the person is telling you so the conversation should move on. I did suggest at one stage, in exasperation, because he clearly did not know, that if my colleague already knew this information then there was no point in continuing with the meeting. He was quite shocked because that is not what he meant at all.

He was simply using a translation of *wo dong le* 我懂了 into English. Literally this is 'I know what you mean', but he had truncated it to "I know" which implied he was already familiar with the problem and its solutions. Now he just says "I understand" and I know he understands the progress of our discussion.

On my end, I also use the literal translation of 'I understand' *wo ming bai le* 我明白了 in meetings. Previously I used the technically correct phrase, as suggested in several phrase books, *wo ting dong* 我听懂, meaning "I can comprehend what you are saying". Or *wo ting bu dong* 我听不懂, meaning "I cannot understand what you are saying". Unfortunately, this phrase has little to do with the content of the conversation. It means the person you are responding to has speech which is understandable. It's a bit like telling a Yorkshire man with a broad accent that you can understand his speech. Obviously, this is somewhat offensive and condescending as a reply to a native Chinese speaker.

There are very important differences between the textbook, or school book language appearing in language programmes and phrase books. It is important to practice your low-level Chinese, but be aware that what you learned from the book may not be the same as language as it is now spoken. Good friends will correct your poor Chinese, just as you will correct a friend's quaint or idiosyncratic English. However, once you move into even slightly more formal circles it is important to get even the simple phrases correct.

These mistakes are amusing, but at times, an irritating problem on a personal level. If we make mistakes like this in these small matters of language, then the potential for significant misunderstanding is increased as the demands of language become more complex. The solution is to make full use of your translator or interpreter to ensure what you say is what you actually mean to say.

Of course, this is not so helpful when you are by yourself, stranded in a sea of Chinese language without a translator in sight.

One of the phrases I most dread hearing in China is *mei wen ti* 没问题 which means 'no problem'. It sounds OK, but in China this phrase has several meanings depending on the situation. You have to decide if it really means 'no problem' or if it means there is a problem, or even a really big problem.

I was reminded of this in Beijing, travelling in a taxi with a driver who was clearly lost but unwilling to admit it. In China I have found myself in similar situations with staff describing a business problem, or with hotel staff attempting to restore an internet connection.

Sometimes you are lucky. *Mei wen ti* really means the person can take care of the problem easily or they can really find the office address in Chaoyangmen without stopping several times to ask for directions from other taxi drivers.

It is more dangerous when *mei wen ti* actually means there is a problem the person cannot solve. He says *mei wen ti* because he doesn't want to admit he cannot solve the problem. In any culture there are many people who do not like to admit they cannot do something, but in China, this can be much more embarrassing, particularly if you are supposed to know. Such as a taxi driver getting lost in the days before WeChat maps. Here, not knowing means a significant loss of face as the angry foreigner gets out of the cab when finally reaching the hotel. Often people will say *mei wen ti* just to buy themselves time before they admit they are lost, or cannot solve the problem.

The worst example was when I arrived in Hangzhou late one night. I gave careful instructions to the driver because there are two hotels with similar names. *Mei wen ti* the driver assured me. *Wo ming bai le* — I understand — he said when I insisted. I was not confident he understood but unfortunately, I was coming down with swine flu at the time and didn't have the energy to argue and take the next taxi in line. Despite my efforts to stay alert, I passed out in the back of the taxi.

Of course, we arrived at the wrong hotel, but my driver had already left when I realised the mistake. In this case *mei wen ti* became a *da wen ti* — big problem.

A solution to the problem of how to assist lost drivers came when I was in a taxi travelling to my friend's house in Haidian, a suburb of Beijing. It was before the time of WeChat maps. Within a kilometre, the driver took a wrong turn. I said nothing, assuming he was taking a short cut I was unaware of. He drove with confidence until the quality of the road deteriorated. Subsequently, we found ourselves travelling along back roads, past areas marked for demolition, where bikes outnumbered cars, and fat rats and thin cats roamed freely. When we stumbled across a multi-lane road, he eagerly turned onto it, but I knew we were going in the wrong direction. We were supposed to be travelling towards Xiang Shan mountain, not away from it.

Now I had a problem. My problem was how to help the taxi driver solve his problem without him losing face. If I had asked him if he knew where he was going, his answer was sure to be "Of course. No problem". And because admitting he was lost would be an even greater loss of face, he would resist any temptation to bring out a map, or pull up beside another taxi and ask for directions.

The solution was to create a situation where he could solve his problem without losing face. I commented, "My friend's home is really difficult to find. I often cannot get there easily. I am sorry, my directions are not good. I will give her a call and she will tell you how to find her home".

I transferred the cause of the problem — it's difficult to find — and provided a solution that did not require the driver to show his ignorance — I would call my friend. This way the driver did not lose face and I could also get to my destination in reasonable time. He also probably appreciated that I understood what he really meant when he said *mei wen ti* — no problem.

The solution is easy when one is in a taxi, but may be much more difficult in other business situations. Still, the challenge remains the same: understand if *mei wen ti* really means there is a problem, or even a big problem. If this is the case, then structure your response in a way to allow the other person to save face by finding a solution, rather than to do so by ignoring the problem.

The final phrase of frustration is *kan qing kuang* 看情况 — depending on how the situation develops. My work involves presentations at conferences and seminars, sometimes alongside other speakers. Keeping a conference running to schedule is a challenge and the Chinese approach is much more flexible than the Western equivalent. In one memorable conference, I ended up with three hands-free microphones draped over my shoulders and clipped to my coat. Despite a pre-conference test, the first microphone did not work when it was time to start the presentation. The second microphone, hastily clipped to my coat lapel also did not work. Finally, the third microphone clipped to the growing cluster on my coat lapel, was successful. I was embarrassed by this failure but the audience took it in their stride.

Sucessful organisation of any type of event in China involves many uncontrollable variables, where important decisions may be in the hands of people external to the event. It is truly a situation of Waiting for the East Wind — *wan shi ju bei, zhi qian dong feng* 万事俱备, 只欠东风. This phrase drawn from the battle of Red Cliff described in *The Romance of the Three Kingdoms* summarises the situation where all is prepared but the execution waits upon just one final factor. Here, *kan qing kuang* is key, it all depends on how the situation develops.

Sometimes though, *kan qing kuang* is used to save face. The person you asked about arrangements really does not have a clue. Rather than lose face and admit this, it is easier to reply *kan qing kuang*. Further questions, even from different angles, will not improve on this answer. Your only solution is to find another person to handle your enquiry.

There is little you can do once the train of events is in motion so I have learned to adjust what I can do as events develop. It allows for relaxation in taxis delayed in traffic; in lengthy delays in aircraft grounded and waiting for take-off clearance; in conferences where events do not start on time and in a myriad of situations where the outcome is unknown. Rather than trying to describe a range of out-comes it is just simpler and more accurate to say *kan qing kuang*.

Well, language habits bring a chuckle but food habits are also an area for potential confusion and in the next chapter, we will discuss them further.

## CHINA BUSINESS BITE

Language translation is not simple. Resolving translation problems always involves face.

# Chapter 22

# A LONG WAY FROM YOUR CHINESE RESTAURANT

China is a long way from your neighbourhood Chinese restaurant. For most of us, the local restaurant or yum cha is our first introduction to Chinese food and dining. However, it provides no introduction to Chinese table manners. I've watched businessmen and cabinet ministers flounder on these basic differences. Travel in China by yourself, or for business, or with a Chinese friend, you will realise how far it is from your favourite Chinese restaurant, in more ways than one.

Chinese restaurants survive in Western cities by altering the flavours and form of the meal so they remain seemingly exotic, but not so exotic as to outrage local tastebuds. This type of compromise is less common in China, so it is useful to be prepared for some differences.

Meals play a much more important role in China than they do in the West. They exemplify the difference between people who live to eat, and people who eat to live. It is not just a reaction to past legacies of famine. In China, meals reflect a genuine love of food, flavour, taste, texture and experience that is a common thread between the most simple and common of meals to the most sophisticated of banquets. Fuchsia Dunlop explores these ideas in *Shark's Fin and Sichuan Pepper*. Individualist cultures have individual plates and meals. The Chinese value relationships, and this is reflected in everybody partaking from a common plate.

Western confusion often starts with the small things, with the water, with the order of serving, the menu variety and perhaps the local eating habits. These are not big obstacles but they provide a rapid guide to your ability to work comfortably in China. We prepare you for some basic surprises so you will be less startled.

When we eat at a Western restaurant, we are usually offered an array of cold-water choices. The first question from the waiter is what type of water you want to drink: still, sparkling, imported or local.

A Chinese waiter will ask what type of tea you would like to drink. Green tea *lü cha* 绿茶 is universal. Black tea *hong cha* 红茶, jasmine tea *mo li hua cha* 茉莉花茶 or flower tea *hua cha* 花 茶 may also be available. It is not much different from the coffee culture of long black, short black, cappuccino or latte. You are rarely offered water because drinking water with a meal is considered to be unhealthy.

Tea is served with a meal for many reasons. Tea is considered to be good for cleansing your palate between bites, or courses, in the same way Europeans use wine. I find *pu'er* 普洱茶 particularly useful in reducing the impact of the oil in Shanghainese cooking. It also reduces the side effects of MSG which is routinely used in Chinese cooking as a flavour enhancer.

Tea is preferred to water because it is believed water will dilute the digestive acids in the stomach, making it more difficult to digest the meal and so bring on indigestion. Green tea in particular also has a wide range of other health benefits associated with the polyphenol found in the leaf. Green tea leaves are steamed, which prevents the polyphenol compounds from being oxidised. By contrast, black and oolong tea leaves are made from fermented leaves, which results in the polyphenol being converted into other compounds.

The black tea we consume in the West is what the Chinese call red tea *hong cha* and is far removed from the original fresh tea leaf as so much of the polyphenol goodness is removed in processing. The primary benefit of the British tea drinking habit was to public health. Tea was made with boiled water and as it became a popular drink, there was a massive reduction in water borne diseases in England.

Increasingly, bottled water is available in China, but almost invariably it will be served or sold at room temperature. Many Chinese prefer to drink liquids at room temperature, or warmer liquids such as tea. They feel cold temperature drinks deliver a shock to the internal organs and stomach. Warm fluids are healthier for the body.

Many Chinese beers taste much better at room temperature than when chilled. The Tsingtao beer often served as Chinese beer is actually a German pilsener designed to be consumed cold. It was first manufactured in the German concession area in Qingdao in 1903. Yanjing 燕京, Beijing 北京, Jinling 金陵 and other popular Chinese beer brands are suitable to be consumed at room temperature and taste quite different when chilled. Snow Beer 雪花 and TsingTao 青岛 beers are best served cold.

It is difficult to resist a chuckle on an Air China flight when a Westerner asks for water.

He expects iced water and he gets a glass of hot water. It's a small welcome to the differences in China. His surprise signals it is going to be a long and difficult journey ahead for him. If you really want iced water on the flight then ask for *bing shui* 冰水 because hot water will usually arrive by default.

Drinking hot water is confusing enough, but where is the rice? The initial Western experience of Chinese cuisine is often framed by their local Chinese restaurant. Many Chinese restaurants historically were established by people who left from Southern China, particularly from the Fujian region, so it is the culinary tradition most Westerners are familiar with. The meal starts with rice because Southern China is a rice-based cuisine and has a rice-based economy. Northern China has a wheat-based economy and cuisine. The differences in these agricultural backgrounds are reflected in the structure of meals.

There is a Chinese saying "No meal is complete without rice". The saying has two interpretations. In Southern China it means every meal includes rice as an accompaniment, and an integral part of the meal. Rice is typically served at the start of a meal. In Hong Kong it is virtually impossible to eat a meal that does not have rice served right at the very beginning.

In Northern China, the saying has a different meaning. Here it means a meal is completed, or finished when the rice is served. Northern eating is more cereal-based with wheats, millets and noodles rather than rice. Often the final course of a meal is noodles or rice, and it is served as a final filler. It is polite not to consume the entire bowl to signal you have had more than enough to eat; if you finish it, you will be served more rice.

I have watched many foreign guests, including overseas Chinese guests wordlessly ask "Where is the rice?" The question underscores the need to replace myth and preconception with the reality of modern China. Rice remains a staple, but its position in the culinary order is a variable dependent upon where you find yourself in China. Its appearance or non- appearance at a meal is a gentle reminder that our ideas need constant reassessment when it comes to working with China.

China is a diverse nation, and eating habits vary widely. Not knowing the basics in the important regions makes a Westerner look foolish. If you do not know how to eat, then you are an easy target for a less than perfect business arrangement because a meal is part of business.

This is not just a problem for Westerners. Overseas Chinese who are working in China face a double jeopardy. They are ethnically Chinese so there is a high level of expectation they will know correct behaviours and habits. An inability to speak Chinese is a severe loss of face. An inability to behave correctly at the important business meal is also a severe loss of face. You cannot expect to do business on your terms if you do not know enough to be able to eat on mainland terms.

It was embarrassing to watch two Western guests at our large banquet table make fools of themselves at a business meal in Shenzhen. The incident was simple. In Shenzhen the common habit is to put two teapots on the table. The first teapot has plain hot water. The second has tea. Water from the first teapot is poured into your small rice bowl. This is then used to wash the flat soup spoons, your chop sticks, and also your small plate. When completed the washing water is poured into a central bowl which has also been placed on the table. This is not a finger bowl.

A Singaporean Chinese took the first teapot and politely poured water into everyone's tea cups. The first Westerner made comments about weak tea. The second drank the water as if it was tea. Knowing the Shenzhen habit, others at the table poured the teacup water into their bowls and washed the eating utensils. Once completed, the teacups were filled with tea from the second teapot which actually held tea.

Another Singaporean Chinese then used the remaining water in the washing-up teapot to top up the teapot which contained tea. This was another embarrassing mistake. One of the other guests from Beijing politely asked the waitress — *fu wu yuan* 服务员 — to bring fresh tea and take the previous two teapots away.

In Singapore and Hong Kong, the female wait staff are called *xiao jie* 小姐, which translates to 'Miss'. In Shenzhen and Shanghai, the term is also slang usage for prostitute so it should be used with caution in a restaurant. You can often tell who is from Hong Kong by listening to how they address the wait staff.

To catch a waiter's attention, just lift your arm to around head height, and wave your hand as if you are patting a dog. Wait staff are not blind, and they will quickly come to your assistance, although there may be some jostling to 'nominate' someone to deal with the foreigner.

At a higher-end restaurant, using this washing procedure for utensils is deeply insulting to the host and the restaurant. If you are not sure of the correct procedure, always try to avoid doing something first. Watch how the locals eat and follow their pattern. This would have saved face for the Singaporeans and prevented the two Westerners from acting foolishly.

If you allow it to, China will always challenge your thinking. Three separate but related incidents reinforced these challenges. In Beijing, I quickly gathered up some Sichuan snacks as a gift for a Chinese friend in Singapore. I did not take sufficient care or thought and purchased some spicy beef. Later she reminded me that her strand of religious faith prevented her from eating beef.

Whilst in Beijing, I had a casual meal with friends. His strand of religious beliefs meant pork was off the menu, despite some very enticing dishes. As always, we deferred to his wishes and selected a wider range of mushroom, tofu and vegetable dishes, along with mutton and seafood. Although it was a small restaurant, the menu offered enough diversity to build a complete meal around his, and our, dietary preferences.

In Singapore, I joined some of our staff for a casual lunch. The group was a mixture of Singaporean Chinese, mainland Chinese, Filipino, Indian and Malay. It included people whose only dietary restriction was the size of the plate, and others who were quite strict vegetarians. The menu, again at a small restaurant, contained enough variety of choice so no one went hungry.

Often, we have the idea, imported from Southern China and Hong Kong that "Chinese people will eat anything that flies apart from airplanes; anything that swims, apart from submarines; and anything that has legs, apart from tables". This is quaintly funny, but terribly incorrect.

Yet this has permutated much of our thinking about Chinese food.

When arranging a dinner for a delegation, we spend much time thinking about the number of courses to be served, but often have little awareness of the reason behind such variety. Often, choices are constrained by menus prepared with local customers in mind, rather than mainland visitors.

There are two challenges here. The first is to bring an extra dimension to our own thinking. It is not safe to assume Chinese guests will eat anything. Paradoxically, it is often not polite to ask about dietary requirements as Chinese guests are accustomed to having a wide range of choices in a menu, or in dishes served at the table in all but the smallest of restaurants. This allows them to unobtrusively select food consistent with their requirements or beliefs. It may come as an unpleasant surprise to find such choices are not available and the result is a hungry guest.

The second is a challenge to our local Chinese restaurants in Western countries to lift their game, sometimes quite dramatically, so the provision of their services gives good face to us and the restaurant itself as hosts. They can do so by providing a much wider variety of selections that go beyond the same meat served with six different combinations of sauce. It is now more common for chefs to have come directly from China, and restaurateurs can improve their performance by listening to their chefs rather than forcing them into the constraints of localised Chinese cooking and menus. They improve their service by simply making quality Chinese tea available instead of the repugnant sticks and leaves all too often served as a generic Chinese tea.

Are these big issues? If you are a tourist, it just confirms the Chinese preconceptions of your ignorance and it doesn't matter. If you are trying to do business, it simply shows you do not understand the situation you are in. It makes you ripe for exploitation and for business on less than favourable terms. The regions of China are very different from each other. There are advantages in understanding these local differences because it smooths the way business is done and relationships are built.

## CHINA BUSINESS BITE

Eating plays a more central role in Chinese life than in the West. The deviation curve from your local Chinese restaurant to even a mid range restaurant in China is large. Be prepared to watch and emulate.

# Chapter 23

# EATING EXPECTATIONS

Our expectations of a Chinese meal are often rudely shaken in China. Chinese expectations of a meal when they visit as a business delegation are also often rudely shaken. There are two possible responses to this situation. First is the response that the Chinese delegation is coming to Australia, or Rome, or New York so they should adapt to the way we do things. That's fine if you wish to ignore the obligations of hosting, spurn the basis of a culture based more around food than ours and send a message that you really just want their investment money and not their friendship. It's a great way to build an exploitative business relationship where trust is low on both sides.

The second response is to accommodate differences to maximise opportunities. Our recommendation is to be a good host, to extend the hand of friendship and create an environment where business is truly a co-operative venture. Understanding Chinese expectations around meals takes us a long way towards this destination. It doesn't mean eating Chinese food, but it does mean eating in the Chinese style.

How important is food? A Singapore Chinese friend talks of his time at university in the south of the United States during the late 1970s. He would ride a bicycle three miles in winter snow to eat fried rice. We should never underestimate the importance of food in a Chinese environment and with that importance comes a range of expectations that form a background to all business and friendship.

The Chinese conference and business delegation market is large. There is increasing demand for conferences involving Chinese businesses and Chinese representatives. These are visiting Chinese delegations, business groups, or Chinese on-site representatives of business. They are foreign-born Chinese and they bring with them a different set of expectations.

Understanding these expectations is important. We can choose to meet these expectations, or ignore them but it needs to be a conscious decision. The real damage is done when we are not aware of these expectations and so we are unaware of our failure to measure up. The result is an unsatisfactory conference or delegation hosting.

But, you may object, they are in my country, so the conference attendees should adapt to our conditions. This is a very valid point. These are not Chinese conferences in a foreign country. They are just events that include Chinese guests. Whilst we do not want to detract from the American, or Australian or European experience, there are ways to make the experience more enjoyable and comfortable for the Chinese guest.

Catering for Chinese in a Western environment can only be an attempt to replicate a Chinese banquet. At one extreme you can host a Chinese banquet. The food will not be the same as in China, but it's the format of the meal that is more important. It's the opportunity to share. Western formats with a single individual plate of food do not create the social atmosphere that is at the core of a shared Chinese meal.

A home-grown Chinese banquet is not always appropriate and guests may also want to sample your local food. The intention is to create the conditions where it is easiest for the guests to appreciate the best food and service the host can provide.

It is so easy to do things badly, even at a government and other high-level functions. A recent high-level function held in Parliament House included many high level Chinese political and business guests. Many were visiting Australia for the first time. The function catering was well intended, serving Australian seafood, beef and fresh produce. The execution of this catering was not so good; it failed to give face to the host and detracted from the event. Highlighting problems is a first step. Coming up with solutions is a more important step.

Food was served as alternate drops. This is a common Western catering approach and is usually fish or a very large chunk of beef or a large serving of chicken. All the Chinese at my table wanted fish as Chinese are not large beef eaters and beef requires more skill with a knife and fork. This request created confusion with the curt response that it was not possible.

Suggested solution: If alternate drop catering is unavoidable then balance the drops with three quarters fish and one quarter beef or chicken. Alternatively, does it really take much more effort to offer just fish for the tables of Chinese guests rather than apply the alternate drop approach? This has the advantage of allowing guests to eat local fish and use chopsticks to do so. The flavours, presentation and freshness of the Western meal are effectively presented in a way easily enjoyed by the guests.

This was a diplomatic event of national importance, but no chopsticks were provided in the place settings. It was embarrassing to watch some senior executives struggle with a knife and fork even though fish is much easier to handle than beef. In the reverse situation, in China, Western guests who are uncomfortable with chopsticks are readily provided with knife and fork. This option was not available at this event.

Suggested solution: Make sure chopsticks are available at all place settings, simply placed beside the Western cutlery. Guests choose which they prefer to use but make sure they are not cheap disposable chopsticks as I have seen provided at a 5-star Western hotel. This is the equivalent of giving Western guests a plastic knife and fork at a Chinese banquet. Having chopsticks available solves a host of problems.

No provision was made for vegetarians. Being vegetarian is not usually a lifestyle choice in China. It is usually a religious restriction. One guest ate only his serving of vegetables and some pumpkin soup, leaving the rest of the food untouched. Understandably hungry, he later had to look for more food options separately at an outside restaurant.

Suggested solution: Make sure vegetarian options are available.

Dessert was served as two platters of finger food in the form of small pastries. They were left untouched and uneaten by Chinese guests because it is impolite to take food from a common plate with your fingers.

Suggested solution: If desserts are served on a platter, then provide small forks, or toothpicks, so the food can be 'speared' and brought to individual plates for eating.

Tea was absolutely unavailable until after dessert was served and when served, only a single cup was available. No refills. Chinese guests asked for tea and their comments in Chinese about its unavailability did not reflect well on the 5-star hotel service supposedly provided by Parliamentary catering.

Suggested solution: Tea is served as soon as people sit down, and cups are refilled constantly. Not having tea available is not an option for a dinner with Chinese guests.

Only cold water was available. For some unaccountable reason, the orange juice did not have ice so many Chinese guests drank the orange juice and ignored the ice-cold water.

Suggested solution: Make sure hot water is available at tables, or at the very least, warm water is available for guests.

As host you have a limited time to make a good impression. Unfortunately, it is much easier to make a bad impression if details, which may appear less important to us, are overlooked. It's the detail and the unexpected importance of some details, that can cause significant damage or provide significant advantage.

Other details of behaviour are less obvious. You have a Chinese delegation in town and you have a choice. There is the formal conference, a voluntary tour on which most Chinese delegates are going, and a dinner. You can attend two of these events, and for the one you do not attend, you must send a junior office delegate. Which two events should you attend?

From a Western perspective the answer is simple. You go to the conference and the dinner, and send a junior delegate from your office on the tour.

From a Chinese perspective the answer is very different. The junior delegate should attend the conference and you should go on the voluntary tour and attend the dinner. It is best if you can attend the opening session of the conference, and then make a polite departure.

So, what is the reasoning behind this?

Conference papers have been prepared and circulated. There will be no surprises, particularly from the Chinese side as they will work from prepared and pre-approved material. This is the presentation of conclusions already agreed upon. The conference is for delivering messages to middle management. It is not about business decisions.

Attending the dinner is essential. This is an opportunity to show your skill and consideration as a host or guest. There will be agreements to confirm and it is a test of goodwill. You must attend and sit at the head table.

Participating in the voluntary tour is essential because this is your opportunity to talk in private, to build relationships and to play the perfect host. It's even more important if senior members of the delegation have chosen to go on the tour. This tour is only in part about seeing the sights. From a Chinese perspective it is the perfect opportunity to discuss issues outside of the formal framework which is focussed on presenting agreed solutions rather than on free-flowing discussion.

Participation in the tour is an opportunity to show that you as a host, respect and value the friendship and relationship. Send an office junior and it shows you do not wish to develop a more personal relationship which is the foundation of extended business. If this is your intention, then sending an office junior is fine. If it is not your intention, then not attending sends the wrong type of message.

Your participation should supplement the tour guide. Point out your favourite parts of the tour, explain why they are significant. Be the gracious and caring host and it will yield dividends. The dinner will be more productive and business will develop more smoothly.

There is one additional factor which Westerners overlook. After the dinner it is not uncommon to suggest a short walk — *san bu* 散步 — with the important guests. This is believed to be good for digestion but it is also an invitation to talk in private and show your concern as a host. This may be a walk that takes the guest back to his hotel, even if it is 10 or 15 minutes away. At the very least, you should accompany the guests to the sidewalk and ensure they are safely in a taxi.

Hosting a delegation is an opportunity to be a good host, but the Chinese expectations of what makes a good host are different to

Western expectations. You improve your business by understanding the Chinese expectations.

## CHINA BUSINESS BITE

Hosting is the foundation of business relations because it reveals much about your character, your consideration and your willingness to work together. It is not a chore added to the main business of the delegation or the conference. It is a core part.

# Chapter 24

# CASE STUDY — THE CHINESE ARE COMING

Contributing author: Lisa O 'Donoghue*

Western visitors to China are overwhelmed by the hosting given to guests with lavish meals, tours and attention. When the Chinese come to visit your country, they are frequently underwhelmed by the attention given to guests. Managing expectations and providing an appropriate level of hosting is a challenge. How you handle this, and often it's a short notice, has a significant impact on the success of business development.

The same applies when you chaperone a business delegation travelling to China. It is a substantial challenge to manage Western expectations in a foreign country. We give you a checklist at the end of this chapter.

It starts when you receive a call from your potential Chinese business or investment partner. He is coming to town and bringing a senior government official from his province, a number of business managers, a technical team, his wife and an interpreter. You have 48 hours to prepare for his trip. Where do you start?

Looking after Chinese visitors is a complex task. The visit is a crucial part of doing business with Chinese and takes you one step closer to closing the deal. But this is not as simple as developing a programme for your Western counterparts. Developing a visit programme for the Chinese requires greater planning, time and resources. The Chinese visit is a test of the value you place on the business and if you fail you may just lose the deal.

A programme for the Chinese visitor requires comparatively greater time, resources and commitment from your organisation than required for hosting a Western business delegation. Office colleagues or managers do not always understand how this fits into a Chinese investment attraction strategy. For colleagues with little China experience, their lack of understanding leads to these questions.

- Why do we have to eat Chinese food when they are here?
- Why don't they speak English when we know they can?
- Why do we have to pick them up from the airport?
- Why do we spend so much time to look after them every minute of the day?

It is critical to build relationships to successfully do business in China. Relationships in China go far deeper than at home and are the necessary foundation for the commitments you will make. There are many barriers to building relationships in China, including the sheer distance between countries and the need to build trust. Developing a relationship in China requires valuable face to face time. Frequent visits by both parties are an important part of this process. The ultimate way to build trust, confidence and your relationship is by ensuring your Chinese business partner has a successful visit whether it be their first or fifth.

When you develop a programme for your Chinese visitors the questions your office colleagues should be asking are:

- How can I build the relationship?
- How can I show my loyalty?
- What can I do to look after my business partner and his delegation?
- How can I build trust to do business in the future?

The Chinese delegation usually has a number of unique requirements and expectations. Those requirements demand a visit programme that focuses on their activities 24/7. It is important you plan activities for your Chinese guests from the moment they get off the plane to the moment they depart to return to China. This is essential for the first-time visitor but it also remains important for experienced Chinese visitor.

The 24/7 programme is intensive but it is a highly recommended approach to ensure the visit is smooth and successful. The visit is an integral part of developing a relationship with your potential Chinese partner. If their memories include trouble finding your office, struggling with food choices, or filling in idle hours with nothing to do, then this will have a negative impact on their visit. This negative perception may further impact you and your potential to do business.

The first step to developing a successful 24/7 programme is to develop a Chinese visit checklist. It may sound like a simple step but it is a vital step to cover all the items you need to address before, during and after the visit. The essential headline items include:

- Who and why
- Point of contact
- Mirror the hospitality

Who is coming and why are they coming? Chinese delegations come in all shapes and sizes. This includes state-owned enterprises, privately owned enterprises, government officials, middle men, wives, cousins and the accompanying shoppers. Each group has its own objectives and requires your full-time focus. Your success comes from gauging the make-up of the group and meeting their individual requirements. Pay attention to each group in the context of the bigger picture and the way it helps you meet your business goals.

Once you have received the list of delegates, determine the importance of the visit by establishing their seniority. Will you be hosting the Chairman, a government official or a technical team?

The Chairman or leader only comes to visit when the Chinese organisation is ready to pursue investment. The lower levels of Chinese management come on earlier visits and do the initial ground work. Their objectives in the early visits are to gain approval and give their leader confidence that the business objectives are achievable.

For the state-owned enterprises, it is important for their provincial government leaders to take part in the investment process and build their own government to government connections. These government connections often take the form of co-operation activities and Memorandum of Understanding agreements between government departments.

Visiting management, research or technical teams, may not have the decision-making power of the Chairman but they have just as much power in stopping, delaying or frustrating the investment process. They usually make a number of visits to build the case they need to present in China. They often need to overcome language difficulties, particularly technical language, and Western business processes in order to fully understand and recommend the investment project.

There will always be a point of contact with every delegation, although it may not be the person who sends you the initial emails. It is essential to identify this contact person and develop good relations. This might be a person you do business with regularly. It might be the person they call the 'interpreter'. This contact is the most important person for you because they provide key information on their delegation's objectives. They are your sounding board for developing the programme, from the logistical details to the appropriate type of leisure activities and to what type of gift you should give.

Hospitality is a mirror of your intentions. Think back at how you were treated when you first visited your Chinese partner in China. Did they pick you up at the airport? Were you wined and dined at a famous Peking Duck restaurant? Were you given a memorable gift? Did they take you to the Great Wall of China? The way you were treated is a measure of the importance they attach to your business relationship. This importance should be mirrored when they visit you.

The Chinese are wonderful hosts and, in many cases, it is difficult to match their hospitality. Creating a visiting programme that attempts to mirror their hospitality will guide you in organising activities valued by Chinese. It may not be as extravagant as the Peking Duck dinner or as exquisite as the Chinese vase you received but it will be well received because it shows you have taken time to consider their well-being. This is the intangible aspect of tangible face.

Take care to avoid the obvious error of giving a gift stamped on the bottom with "Made in China". It is no laughing matter. I have seen this done, and deals become so much harder to finalise as a result.

Understanding Chinese protocol and culture is essential to the success of your Chinese visit programme. Stepping outside these protocols and cultural practices may cause serious embarrassment, negatively impact on their visit experience and harm your relationship.

In your home environment it can be difficult to meet the expectations of Chinese guests. There are some ways to overcome these difficulties and deliver a successful Chinese visit programme.

Start with building connections with your local Chinese restaurants. The dining experience in China is difficult to match outside of China. The quality and authenticity of Chinese food, private dining experience and service capabilities are difficult to achieve for your local Chinese restaurants because they need to cater for a Western clientele.

By developing good connections with your local Chinese restaurants, you can better meet the requirements of your Chinese visitors. Many local restaurants will enthusiastically embrace the opportunity to develop an authentic Chinese meal. Ignore those that do not share the enthusiasm. Many of the restaurants have Chinese chefs who, when given the opportunity, can serve up dishes from different Chinese provinces. It is always a pleasant surprise for Hunan visitors to be served their local delicacies in a foreign city.

When the Chinese come to town, it is an opportunity to show and return the respect necessary to build a firm foundation for business and investment.

## Taking a Delegation to China

Increasingly, foreign delegations are heading to China and that's an entirely new minefield. There are all the usual considerations of guest and host discussed above, but there are additional considerations. This checklist builds on the issues raised in previous chapters.

1. Caution is required with setting flight schedules and connections. Leave several hours additional buffer for domestic connections within China. Delays are more frequent in second and third tier cities. When there are major national flight disruptions then first tier city flights are cleared first. Third tier cities are the last to be cleared. I co-hosted a trade delegation of political and business leaders. Due to a typhoon in Guangzhou, our flights from Qingdao were cancelled. Against my advice, the State leaders' Chief of Staff booked flights via tier 3 cities when our direct flights were cancelled. The schedule looked good on paper, but what should have been a 4.5 hour journey took 30 hours.

2. Engage professional translators for delegation leaders. A good translator enhances business. A poor translator kills business. Some official trade departments like to hire translators on the cheap with university students. This is usually because delegation organisers say the cost of engaging good translators is too high, particularly when political leaders are involved and there is public pressure to reduce costs. We have preferred translators whom we fly around China as required.

3. Larger conference rooms are preferred so that translator booths are well separated from the audience. If 100 people are expected, then book room with 150 guest capacity.

4. Go for simultaneous translation in forums and conferences. This increases the amount of content that can be delivered.

5. Be prepared to pay for some services in cash or by WePay transfer. This includes freelance translators, unscheduled meals, taxis, equipment hire and car hire. In Qingdao we had booked a delegation dinner at a restaurant 300 metres from the hotel. Unfortunately, it was pouring when the time came to depart. A mini bus belonging to a different delegation dining at the hotel was parked in the forecourt. In return for a small cash payment, the bus was unofficially hired for the 300-metre journey.

6. Decide in advance the seniority order of the delegation. This can ruffle some feathers so care is required. Provide this to the Chinese side for all meetings. Make sure the delegation knows the seniority order and takes appropriate seating etc.

7. Named seating should be used for every seat and every table at every meeting, function or conference. If you have invited Chinese guests, then make sure they have named seating.

**CHINA BUSINESS BITE**

Work with Chinese colleagues to help you to see 'through Chinese eyes' and hear 'through Chinese ears'. It gives you an indication of what the other side is thinking and feeling and helps meet or manage their expectations.

*Lisa O'Donoghue is former Senior Business Development Manager, Department of Mines and Energy, Northern Territory Government of Australia*

# Chapter 25

# CHINA CASE STUDY — BEIJING BUSINESS TABLE MANNERS

Eating in China is rarely relaxed as you and your actions are always under scrutiny in an endless quest to reveal something of your character. These notes apply to a mid-level business meal arranged in Beijing in northern China where the manners and habits are quite different from southern and western cities.

We are accustomed to the southern Chinese eating style so we can easily get by in Hong Kong and Shanghai. Northern dining style is different and we put ourselves at a disadvantage if we do not know the differences in expectations. This summary guide is not for a banquet, nor for a meal with friends. It's the arrangements you can expect to encounter at a mid-level business meal in Beijing. It is also a suitable guide for when you are hosting a delegation from northern China in your home country. This is sophisticated dining and it is essential for all business.

How important is this? The big issues are the issues that can really hurt and cause lasting harm. This includes ignoring face, slighting senior officials, losing your temper and embarrassing a counterpart business partner. These notes deal with smaller issues but it is important to be aware of these issues. You score valuable points with this knowledge, earn face, gain respect and get ahead of your competition. This breaks down pre-conceptions about Westerners and smooths the way. Don't ignore the apparently little things. These may be trivial to you but they can be very important to your Chinese counterparts.

Remember the meal will always be in a private room. No one will discuss real business in an open room. Remember also that there is no free seating. Know where all your important guests will sit, and if you are the important guest, know where you will sit. The place for the most important person is often marked with a table napkin standing higher than the others or of a different colour.

If you are a guest, then pre-brief the host organiser so they know you prefer Chinese food. It means everyone is comfortable and you will avoid some very unpleasant attempts at Western food created in good faith by Chinese restaurants. If you have allergies, let this be known in the planning stage of the meal.

As an important guest, you are a big person so expect to be waited on. You enter the room first. If you are not the main guest, then enter the room in what you think is appropriate hierarchal order. Don't defer to wait staff but wait for seat allocation. Your translator sits beside or just behind you.

If you are hosting a dinner in China then life is a little more complicated. Always use a private dining room. They are readily available in all but the smallest of restaurants. Seek advice from your Chinese staff. Don't have any staff? Then locate the restaurant first and ask for their advice. Make sure the menu has pictures so you have some idea of what you are ordering. Use local advice to pre-decide the courses. Ask wait staff what they have seen other groups order for this type of meal. Arrive early and decide the menu in advance before guests arrive.

The host faces the door with the important guest on his right. If you are the host, then make a show of menu selection and discussion when the guests arrive even if you have already pre-ordered. It shows you are concerned about their comfort.

Northern table place settings consist of a bowl, a small plate, chopsticks and a flatbottomed spoon. Unlike the southern Chinese custom, the bowl is not placed on the small plate. It is placed to one side and used for soup, or later in the meal, for noodles and rice. We assume you are proficient with chopsticks, or that you have practised before you came to China. If your skill is moderate then people will politely exclaim "You can use chopsticks". If your skill is quite good then you will be complimented "You use chopsticks very well". When your skill is equal to that of a lifelong user then no comment is required.

For northern Chinese meals, it is useful to learn to use chopsticks and a flat bottom spoon together correctly. Chopsticks are used to take a small morsel of food from the main serving dish. Food is generally put down on the small plate first before it is picked up again and transferred to your mouth. Alternatively, for slippery foods or those that are difficult to pick up, transfer them to the spoon held in the left hand and then move them to the small plate. Only two or three bites of food are placed on the small plate at any one time. When these are finished, more food is placed on the plate. It is considered impolite to take food from the main serving dish and put it directly in your mouth. Western style has all the food required for the meal on one plate. Chinese style is one or two mouthfuls from a single dish on the plate, and then when eaten, replenished from another dish. Food is transferred to and eaten from the plate, not from the bowl, with the exception of the last dish, usually rice or noodles.

The corner of the table napkin is placed under the plate and draped over your midriff. The napkin is not placed in your lap, or if it is, it is quickly placed under the plate. Watch how people behave in this situation. You can pick out northern Chinese people in any crowd just by the way they use their table napkins.

Generally, a small box of tissues is also available on the table. Use these to keep your mouth clean. Use these also to clean your chopsticks should they become too greasy or sticky. Plates will be cleared regularly by staff so the edge of the plate is used for scraps.

Courses tend to follow a strict order: cold dishes, fish, meat, vegetables, rice/noodles, soup, fruit. As a guest it is good to eat a small amount of everything but be careful of leaving an empty plate for too long. An empty plate will be filled — endlessly — by your host on the assumption that you are still hungry. Rice or noodles are normally the last course in a Northern meal unless a particular dish is traditionally served with rice. Pungent Hunan cooking often comes with a small terracotta bowl of compacted rice. It is designed to soak up some of the excess oils.

It is impolite to take the last serving from the main serving bowl, but if you are offered it, then it is polite to accept. As a guest, good food will be passed to you by the host — with chopsticks. Sometimes public chopsticks may be used, but more frequently, the host will use his own chopsticks. It's a sign of respect, so get used to it. Do not recoil in horror or disgust.

Do not ask what food you are eating. You may not like the answer. Something that was quite pleasant may now stick in your craw, or threaten to fight its way back up your throat. The lazy Susan is rotated clockwise. As a guest you should not move this. As a host, keep the lazy Susan moving regularly as your guest's plate is emptied. It shows you are attentive to the guest's needs.

Just as there is an etiquette for Western cutlery, there is also a well-developed etiquette for chopsticks. Most of these are don'ts, and they include:

Don't pick up any dropped food from the table and eat it. Leave it where it is, or gently nudge it under the lip of the lazy Susan. Eating food from the table is considered most unhygienic and disgusting.

Don't root around in a dish to find nice morsels that you like. Use this as a test of your chopstick skills to select the bit you want and to avoid the bits you do not like.

Don't pick one piece then drop it back in the serving plate so you can change to a different morsel.

Don't let your chopsticks become covered with food juice or residue. Use the tissues provided, not the table napkin, to clean them.

Don't wave your chopsticks or use them to point.

Don't use chopsticks like forks. You may see others use a chopstick in each hand to separate food but they have a knowledge and skill that you do not.

Don't lick or suck your chopsticks.

If you are hosting a Chinese delegation in your country then there are some things you can do to make the eating experience more enjoyable.

Provide a choice of chopsticks or knife and fork at every table place setting.

Pre cut food, such as steak, so it can be eaten with chopsticks.

Put finger food on a central platter with tongs or chopsticks so it can be transferred to individual plates without picking up by hand.

Avoid, or clearly label cheese dishes.

Make hot water or warm water available. Avoid chilled water.

Where possible have seating labelled for business meetings.

Horror stories around Chinese drinking abound. The preference for *maotai* 茅台 or *bai jiu* 白酒 — clear grain-based liquors with a taste and smell most Westerners find unpleasant — is compounded with invitations to indulge in heavy drinking. There is a belief a drunk person will reveal their true character.

You may decide to go absolutely teetotal for your entire trip to China. Telling your host beforehand you are unable to drink alcohol for health reasons is an acceptable excuse. Getting caught out in a lie when you are seen drinking somewhere else is unforgivable. If you choose to drink then here are a few strategies.

Beer or wine on the table is not for drinking Western style. It is mainly used for toasting, rather than slaking thirst. This is also different from southern China. The host buys beer. The guest never orders another bottle, or asks for more. To do so insults the host by suggesting he is not caring enough.

Beer is usually warm, so it makes more sense to agree to Chinese beer which is designed to be drunk at room temperature rather than foreign beer which is designed for drinking at a colder temperature.

Drinking has very different objectives to the West so the bottle does not have to be finished when the meal ends. Glasses do not have to be emptied when the meal ends, although there may be some pressure to do this. Toasting is initiated by the host, then later, guest to host. The first toast is sometimes *gan bei* 干杯 — literally dry glass. Westerners often interpret this literally, but it is no different from 'bottoms up' or 'cheers'. You do not have to empty your glass.

Like the rest of the meal, this is a test, so sip beer, don't drink it. China is not a place to get drunk at a business meal. Never pour your own beer as this suggests the host is neglecting you. If you are the host then fill other guests' glasses first, or get wait staff to do this.

Toasts are always done with glass to glass touching. If it is not possible at a large table, then tap the edge of the lazy Susan with your glass once or twice. The senior person's glass is held highest in a toast. If you are the senior guest, it is polite to try to keep the lip of your glass lower than the host's when touching glasses for the toast. Respect is shown by using two hands on the glass when drinking with another. The fingers of the left hand are placed under the bottom of the glass while drinking.

Beer or alcohol is only sipped during a toast. If you pick up your glass, you should toast, even if it is only the person beside you. In northern meals it is not polite to drink alone. This is a very Beijing habit and not one observed in Shanghai and southern China.

Red wine in particular is used primarily for toasting rather than drinking with a meal. When used for toasting the wine is sipped, so a single glass may last for 5 or 6 rounds of toasting. Even if you do not drink, it is polite to accept a glass of red wine. When the time comes to toast, then simply go through the motions without drinking. It is polite and acceptable.

If you want to drink because the food is too spicy, then drink tea — it is easier than water and staff will always refill your cup — but they will not usually refill a water glass

*Gan bei* — dry glass — may be an invitation to a drinking competition. Try to avoid participating. You can respond with *sui bian* 随便 or *ru nin suo yuan* 如您所愿, both of which mean 'As you wish' and indicate a polite refusal of the invitation to drink heavily.

I cannot emphasise this enough: *gan bei* is not a Western style last man standing competition. It is meant to be an assessment of your true character. Whilst you are busy getting drunk and your Chinese counterpart is also getting drunk, remember that their translator is sober and watching you. Later on, they will report their assessment of you and any of your antics.

Tea is a salvation at a meal. You can drink as much as you want whenever you want. Drink this at any time without the need to toast. It's a lifesaver. If you are not drinking, then you can also accept and return toasts using your tea cup.

Tea is sometimes served in a lidded cup. Use the lid of the cup to keep leaves in the tea cup when you drink it. Men use one hand, holding the cup and shifting the lid slightly leaving just a small gap to capture the tea leaves. If you want more hot water or tea, shift lid to one side of the cup. When you fill your own cup, always fill others first, even just a little, before refilling your own. When tea is poured for you signal thanks by lightly tapping your index finger on the table two or three times.

Earlier we noted a list of don'ts but we also need to mention some acceptable Chinese behaviours which often are not acceptable to Westerners:

- It is okay to slurp noodles — a habit many Westerners find intensely irritating.
- Snuffling and sniffing is okay. Blowing your nose on your handkerchief at the table is not okay. If you need to do this, use a tissue and turn away from the table. Better still, leave the room.
- It is okay to bring the bowl to your mouth so you can move food more easily.
- It is ok to drink or slurp soup directly from the bowl.

The following are a few more pointers for business meals:

- When eating *jiao zi* 饺子 — dumplings — put one onto a spoon and then eat the *jiaozi* off the spoon.
- Beware of *xiao long bao* 小笼包 which contains hot 'soup'. Put one on a spoon, break the edge of the skin with chopsticks, slurp the soup, then eat the dumpling.
- Eat slowly — eating is considered a leisurely experience where taste, flavour, texture, presentation and food quality is to be appreciated.
- If something is not to your taste, spit it onto your chopsticks or spoon, and put it on the edge of the plate.
- Avoid using your fingers to pick up anything. Exceptions include crab claws and pork or mutton ribs. Watch how other people use a combination of chopsticks and fingers to eat and try to emulate.

- If you cannot pick a particular piece of food up with chopsticks and a spoon, then leave it on the edge of the plate.
- Don't chase food if it drops into your lap. Just ignore it and carry on as if nothing has happened. That's what the napkin is for.
- A meal is an invitation to think about doing business. It is not relaxation, even after a deal has been signed. It is not wise to let your guard down because you are still being assessed.
- Safe areas of table conversation include:
  - What are the best areas in the city? People will be proud to tell you.
  - Famous sites nearby. This is an opportunity to get an insider's view.
  - Favourite local food. Just be careful as you may be invited to sample a variety of local favourites that are not really to your taste.
  - Favourite regional food.
  - The host's aspirations for his child.
- Remember to look at the person you are listening to or talking to. Do not look at your translator, or their translator.
- You are a guest so be mindful about the following topics:
  - Tibet — it has been a Chinese province for thousands of years. You might not agree, but this is not the place to argue.
  - Taiwan is part of the mainland. You might not agree, but this is not the place to argue.
  - Tiananmen was caused by a small group of duped agitators. You might not agree, but this is not the place to argue.
  - Mao is a hero who bought China into the modern world.
  - The cultural revolution is not discussed.
  - Current issues in Chinese politics.
- Avoid loud laughter. It is considered impolite.
- Don't tell any jokes — they usually translate very badly.
- Don't tell sexual jokes or make sexual references especially, as this crosses many more boundaries than most Westerners can imagine and it will cause lasting harm to your business relationships.
- When people cover their mouth and laugh at something that is not funny you should understand you have just made a significant error.

- The meal always ends with fresh fruit — it is not polite to take the last piece so offer it to someone else. Even if they decline, do not take the last piece. The end of the meal is signalled with the distribution of toothpicks. Cover your mouth with your hand when using a toothpick. This is not the time for US wild west style toothpick activity.

If you are the host then arrange for bill payment beforehand. If this is the first meal together and you are the guest then ignore the payment discussion or bill checking. Say *fei chang gan xie* 非常感谢 — sincere thanks — to your host personally but quietly as you leave the meal.

The idea that the guest and the host fight over the payment of the bill is a misconception. If you have been invited as a guest then the host expects to treat you as a guest. You insult your host if you fight to pay because it implies you think he doesn't have the capacity to pay. Later if you become good friends, then it is appropriate to indulge in good natured banter about settling the bill.

If it is not clear who is host, or who is guest, then always offer to pay the bill. At the end of the first meal also discuss when you will host a return meal.

Meals end quickly after fruit. *Zou ba* 走吧 or *zou* 走 — literally 'walk' — signals the end of the meal. Meals are not usually followed by long Western style conversations over coffee. If you are the host, then do not linger so your guests can leave.

The meal may be followed by other activities. If you are the guest, always accept an invitation to *san bu* 散步 — stroll — after the meal. This is an invitation to discuss business. If you are the host, decide if it is appropriate to invite guest to *san bu*.

These notes are drawn from a lunch workshop we provide as part of our www.workingwithChina.com services to government and industry. We do not expect you to remember all of these. The intention is to give you a guide to the type of behaviour you can expect to encounter. Business in Beijing has a different flavour to business in Shanghai, Nanjing or Changsha. You are judged on your table manners in Beijing in a way that you are rarely judged in Western countries. The more you know, the better the impression you can create. Just how far you need, or want, to go down the road of Chinese compatibility is a question we look at in the next section.

## CHINA BUSINESS BITES

A Chinese meal is a minefield for the unwary and the uncaring. This is where your business is made, or unmade. If you study nothing else for your trip to China, this is the one thing you cannot afford to avoid.

# Chapter 26

# LITTLE BITES OF LANGUAGE

It is not necessary to learn Chinese to work effectively in China, particularly now that good translation programs are available on WeChat. That said, scrabbling for your phone to keep a conversation going is not really evidence of language fluency.

Knowing some Chinese will give you an advantage. You can follow conversations and confirm translations are correct. But speaking or not speaking Chinese also has a lot to do with face. We think speaking some Chinese or good Chinese, gives us face. It is not always correct.

Face is a concept we find difficult to understand but it is a vital factor in every relationship in China. In southern China, particularly in the major cities, it is slightly less important, or people are more forgiving of Western habits. But in northern China, and Beijing, there is less latitude.

My Chinese language skills are not good enough to allow me to do complete public speaking presentations in Chinese. I do use Chinese when I am speaking in public, but it is kept to a smattering. It is a politeness. In formal functions and dinners where I am a guest, I will use more Chinese, again more as politeness. In informal situations, meals with friends and colleagues, I will use a much wider mixture of Chinese and English. Face is still involved, but it is related to my skill, or lack of it in Chinese, and my dedication to learning. It may be politely acknowledged with the comment *xin ku le* 辛苦了! It means 'you have worked hard, continue to endure and improve'. The face in each situation is different.

When I am speaking as a foreigner, as a foreign expert, or as a representative of Australia, I am expected to speak English. By speaking English, I give face to the country I represent, or to the foreign company I represent. Even if I could speak fluent Chinese, I would not do so in this formal public speaking environment because I lose face. Not because my language skills are inadequate, but because I am not effectively representing my foreign company or country. I am not Chinese, and my country is not Chinese, so why am I not speaking my own language? There is a danger that people will assess you as knowing how to speak Chinese, but not understanding Chinese.

Knowing some Chinese makes it easier to get around, to make simple hotel and restaurant requests, to give instructions to taxi drivers and to participate in informal conversations. The skill is appreciated and admired, and it does give you face in these situations. However, when you put on your public face, speaking Chinese does not always give you face. In fact, it may lose face for you and your company, and even your country.

Working in China is relatively easy. Working *effectively* in China is more difficult and challenging. Often the result, despite our best intentions, is the opposite to what we expect. My regular Beijing hotel is a five-star Chinese hotel, not a Western chain in China. I wanted some printing done so I went to the business centre and I asked correctly in Chinese for the service. Then I gave my room number and I signed the invoice writing my name in Chinese characters. The business office staff looked at the guest register, then at my Chinese signature. In Chinese she told me, "Sorry, the guest in this room is not Chinese. Please write your name in English." I had to re-sign the invoice in English.

Caucasians speaking Chinese can cause confusion in China. I visited my local bank branch in Beijing. Normally you take a ticket from a machine and wait for your number to be called but they had shifted the machine to a different location behind the welcome counter. I went to the counter. "*Ni hao*", I said while I looked around for the ticket machine. "*Qu piao ji zai na? Wo yao qu hao.* 你好。取票机在哪儿？我要取号. Hello. Where is the ticket machine? I need a ticket number".

The young lady saw me as a Caucasian, listened to what I said, and replied in English: "How may I help you?" English was not what I was expecting to hear, so it simply did not register in my mind. Because I had been listening to and speaking Chinese all morning, I automatically replied "*Shen me? Wo ting bu dong.* 什么? 我听不懂。What? I don't understand".

There was a moment of confusion as we both sorted out our languages. She realised my first question was in Chinese — she had expected to hear English — and retrieved the ticket. I realised her reply was in good English — I expected Chinese — and I complimented her in English on her English.

When the Chinese person is all tensed up expecting to hear English it can be confusing when you speak Chinese.

Learning some Chinese, even if its Starbucks Chinese, is an advantage. Starbucks Chinese is used to describe mastery of the basics required to order coffee, a meal, to get around and hold very simple conversations. Learning Chinese is difficult and unless you have a natural ability with languages — and even then — it is going to take a lot of effort and time to become reasonably competent or fluent.

Many researchers are confirming what many people intuitively believed. The most effective learning is situational. This applies particularly to language learning. The classroom, or the language program on your computer, is essential for learning the basics of the language. However, the classroom is not real life so the language learnt in the classroom is stilted and difficult to remember in the field.

If you want to develop your language skills more fluidly, and with less pressure, then it helps to put yourself in the way of opportunity. Singapore is an ideal place for this because it is like the shallow end of the pool. If you make a mistake, you can always revert back to English.

I find taxi drivers the most useful informal language teachers. Where possible I try to select taxis in Singapore with Chinese rather than Malay or Indian drivers. Taxi drivers are often a talkative bunch, happy to share their opinions, their ideas and their stories if the passenger is willing to ask questions and listen. And they are willing to do so all in Chinese.

Unlike wait staff in a restaurant who are busy flitting from table to table, you have the taxi driver to yourself for the full duration of the trip. Break the language ice when you get into the cab, and give directions in Chinese. 'Hello. I want to go to Wheelock Place. *Ni hao. Wo yao qu* Wheelock Place. 你好。我要去 Wheelock Place.' Westerners speaking Chinese, or Westerners speaking not so good Chinese, are usually met with some disbelief. Don't be surprised to see the driver do a double take, but there is a high probability he will return the favour and reply in Chinese.

It is an opportunity to extend your listening and speaking skills in a situational environment. It is usually a standard set of opening questions. "You can speak Chinese? *Ni hui jiang hua yu?* 你会讲华语?" Unless you really are fluent, it is polite, and wise, to reply that you speak only a little Chinese. "*Yi dian dian.* 一点点。" The next question is usually "Where do you come from? Where did you learn Chinese?" You can move beyond these basics to talk about what you like in Singapore, when you are going home and where you work.

These are mixed Chinese and English conversations, but they are conversations without pressure. Unlike in a classroom, these are not specified drills taken out of context, so the 'stickability' of the learning is greater. Taxi drivers, like good teachers, are usually considerate. If they realise they have replied with language complexity greater than your skill level, they will drop it down a notch or two so you can understand.

The real test of your language skill development is when you get into the back seat of the taxi and say a simple "*Ni hao.* 你好". The driver replies in Chinese "*Qu Na li?* 去哪里? Where to?" which indicates he has assumed you are fluent in Chinese from your initial greeting in Chinese.

People are generally delighted when you make an attempt to speak their language and taxi drivers give you the opportunity to practise for an extended period, especially if you are stuck in a jam. The more you practise, the longer the taxi conversations become and the greater your understanding of the language. These are the building blocks of competence and you find them in many places outside of the classroom.

Language practice is essential. A colleague commented that after returning from a trip to China he found no difficulty in holding a short conversation in Chinese with a shop assistant in Singapore. When he returned to the same shop six weeks later the shop assistant greeted him in Chinese, ready to take up the conversation again. To his embarrassment, fresh from six weeks in Australia and not speaking Chinese, he found his Chinese had deserted him.

Acquiring a second language, even at a basic conversational level, is a matter of use it or lose it. So, the key question is how do you 'use it' when you are back in your home country? There are several methods, some more easily practised than others.

The most difficult is to continue with formal Chinese language lessons. This is difficult because by nature these lessons are sequential. You miss a few lessons, and you get left behind in the class. The structure of scheduled lessons also detracts from the spontaneity of practice. It's a set time, rather than a variety of situations. Also, the purpose of formal language training is often very different from the more free-flow nature of everyday conversation.

The same shortcoming applies to using computer software language programs. These are great for honing language skills and revision, but they lack the immediacy of real conversations which veer off in unexpected directions.

The easier method is to practise informally whenever the opportunity arises. Increasingly the wait staff in many Chinese restaurants in Western countries are mainland Chinese students. They are often quite surprised, and delighted, if you speak to them in Chinese. Initially they may not respond and look confused because they expect to hear English when speaking with Westerners. However, try placing your order in Chinese, even if it's limited to '*Gei wo zhe ge he na ge* 给我这个和那个' while pointing to the menu items which means 'Give me this and that'. Or '*Gei wo san shi san hao, he wu shi er hao.* 给我三十三号和五十二号。Give me number 33 and number 52'. This breaks the ice, and depending on the crowd level in the restaurant you may be able to spend more time in conversation. It's the simple questions that open up the conversation. Where is your home? Do you like it here? How long have you been here? It is an opportunity to practise your speaking and conversation skills in an informal and genuine situation outside of a classroom.

Try the same when paying the bill. You will be asked the question in English, but if you respond in Chinese you may find the reply given in Chinese. Get in first, asking *duo shao* qian? 多少钱? How much to pay?' Again, depending on the rush and the crowd, you may find yourself involved in a longer Chinese conversation.

If you make a habit of visiting the restaurant regularly, you may find one or two of the wait staff more than willing to engage you in Chinese conversation. It is one of the methods I use to quickly knock the rust off my language skills when I am in Singapore on my way to Beijing. I go to the same restaurant, Din Tai Fung, and order in Chinese. Many of the staff are from mainland China. The staff know me and use Chinese from the time of first greeting when I request for a table, to repeating my order and directing me to my table when it is ready. It's a quick and comfortable language revision that makes it easier to order drinks and select meal choices on the Air China flight to Beijing.

Just because you are at home, it does not mean there are no opportunities to continue to practise your Chinese speaking and conversation skills. If you seek out the opportunities and use the opportunities then you can limit the rusting of your skills. It is lots of unstructured fun, and it also often gives enjoyment to the Chinese speakers you interact with, who spend most of their time serving monolingual Westerners.

## CHINA BUSINESS BITE

Speaking Chinese is not always an advantage and will not always give you face in a business situation. Practise your Chinese in every appropriate situation possible to improve your speaking and comprehension.

# Chapter 27

# HOTEL PRISON BREAKOUT

Working in Dalian in north China, I was reminded of the difficulty faced by people who are in China by themselves. I bumped into an American colleague who was on his third business event in China. Travelling by himself, he felt the hotel was a type of prison. He was trapped inside by his inability to speak any Chinese, or to read any of the signs.

Travelling by yourself in China is very different to travelling with a tour group. You get more out of the experience if you are prepared to be a little adventurous. The hotel doesn't have to be a virtual prison.

Most four- or five-star hotels have a concierge tour desk. Although they are set up to offer tour and sightseeing information, they will happily help you with other requests. Ask them for directions to the nearest shopping centre. The shopping centre will usually include food outlets, from delis, to restaurants and cafes. These shopping centres are modern, but with Chinese characteristics. The hotel doorman who calls a taxi will happily give the taxi driver your instructions.

Take a photo of the hotel name card with the hotel address printed in Chinese to show to a taxi driver when you want to get back to the hotel. It can all be done by sign language, smiles and shakes of the head if necessary.

The objective is to simply get dropped off at the shopping centre. Use this as an anchor point to explore inside the centre, or to walk the surrounding blocks. The variety of life, of commerce, of activity is fascinating. The photo of your hotel name card is your return ticket to the safety of the hotel so it's a relatively risk-free exercise.

Taxis are ubiquitous, so you are not going to be stranded.

Supermarkets are a great place to shop for food. First, I find it interesting to see what is stocked on the shelves. The vegetables, the food, the preserved food, the range of preserved fruits, the packaged food and other items provide a good guide to living standards and conditions.

More importantly, the supermarkets are a focal point for the equivalent of delis, both inside the supermarket and outside. These are many small food stalls, each specialising in a particular type of food. This is common food, but with a difference. Food on the street may be cheap, but it may also be suspect. Food from these delis is well prepared and higher quality. You can buy and eat with confidence.

Often the food deli area is located in the basement of a department store. You walk through the displays of jade jewellery, gold, high end perfumes and face creams, find the escalator and descend into the Chinese equivalent of a food court.

It is an education just to walk through aisles and see the variety. I did this with my American colleague. I explained the different foods and preparations. The staff behind the counters were amused. I spoke in English to my friend and Chinese to them. We also ended up with a whole range of free samples to taste. It was a good strategy of course, because I felt some obligation to buy small amounts for my friend to try. I ended up buying much more than I needed. Just a bit of this and a bit of that; a few slices of smoked pork, a *jian bing* 煎饼 — a type of crepe pancake with spring onion and egg folded with deep fried crispy bean curd skin, some *hua man tou* 花馒头 flower steamed bread, some fruit, and some other nibbles.

This is cheap eating. It's a few yuan for *man tou*, or pancakes, or roasted pork knuckle. Buy small amounts and try. Speaking Chinese is not required. The offer of food and the selection of food can be done without exchanging words. If it's not to your liking then simply do not eat it. There is no great cost involved, but there is face involved. Always take your order in a bag and take it away to eat. If you don't like the taste you can stop eating it without causing any offence.

Real people do not live in hotels nor do they live in board rooms, private dining rooms or tourist attractions. That's not to say these people are not real, but they are not the ordinary people who inhabit the city. They are a specialised and self-selected group who choose to, or by necessity, interact with foreigners.

As a visitor to a city it is difficult to get a feel for the city outside of the business environment unless you are fortunate enough to develop strong friendships that take you out into the wider world. But alternatives exist when you have spare time and the best alternative is to walk.

This is a common alternative in Europe. Western visitors feel more comfortable with a walk along unknown streets even if it is past midnight in Paris, but far less comfortable in Beijing, Xi'an or Shanghai even if it's in the middle of the day. For many, there is a daunting foreignness heightened by language which is more incomprehensible than French or Italian. The feeling is added to by street and shop signage that is indecipherable even if you possess a smattering of the spoken language. Leaving the hotel unaccompanied can be a real adventure but also provide interesting insight into the lives of real people.

I was reminded of this in Beijing when a scheduled meeting was postponed. I had a few hours to fill and rather than revisit the Summer Palace, or the Temple of Heaven, I decided to take a walk.

It was one of those deceptive Beijing days. Clear blue skies, the touch of oncoming winter, a chill in the air, and then a slice-to-the-bone blast of cold wind sweeping across the northern plains. Not cold enough for snow, and just cold enough to have started to turn the colour of the leaves and sprinkle the ground with paper-like leaves after every gust of wind.

Generally Beijing, and other cities, are constructed on a grid pattern. Using the main road as a reference point, I walked, and then turned down the side roads, turning left and then right and right again to bring me back to the main road reference point. Like knitting loops in a scarf this lets you explore without losing your sense of direction.

You do not have to move far to leave the noise of traffic behind. It is swallowed by the elm trees lining each side of the road. The noise is smothered by the climbing roses on the courtyard fences and absorbed by the thick, but browning grass in the garden beds.

It's a series of vignettes. The shops are smaller and less glamorous than those in the shopping malls. Surprisingly many carry English translations so it is generally clear what the shop is selling. Life on a quiet Sunday afternoon includes friends walking arm in arm, sons and daughters taking parents for a stroll, lovers holding each other more closely than is strictly necessary, young people clustered around MacDonald's, and lurking across the road as always, more are gathered around Kentucky Fried Chicken.

Food is a constant, and restaurants big and small dot the landscape. For many people, eating outside the home is a daily pleasure. Look down the laneways and you might see a chef standing over a wok of boiling water slicing fresh knife-cut noodles from a slab of dough into the hot water. You can join the line for fresh steamed buns, *jian bing*, or steamed dumplings.

China is more than business or tourism. China is also about its people and not just the people you meet formally. Rather than scuttle back to the hotel after a meeting or after a trip to the shopping mall, it is useful to take the opportunity to explore the area on foot. Armed with some snacks, it's a pleasant stroll and exploration of the surrounding blocks and buildings. You will not have the benefit of a tour guide telling you the significance of what you see, but nor will you have the pressure of a schedule.

There are other things to be learned through observation of people in normal activity. The conversations between street vendors and their customers, the disparity between those with money and those who do not have it, the sound of an *er hu* 二胡, the Chinese two string fiddle with a haunting soul of sound being played by an old man huddled under his coat in the winter cold. Be generous, give him a few yuan and some respect.

In Shanghai, it is comfortable to walk under the shade of the European elms transplanted by European colonists in the Western concession areas. It is Paris before post-war commercialisation. Or take a stroll through public parks to watch the calligraphers at work with giant brushes dipped in water. They write ancient poems on the concrete while couples dance to ballroom music in the park and the quiet glow of the evening.

In Dalian, the stroll has a Russian or Eastern European feeling. It's one that is invoked by the architectural features of buildings, the trees and tired grey concrete buckled by snow melt. The old buildings learn against each other, somehow not always quite plumb as if lurching from a *baijiu* hangover.

In Beijing, a walk includes a bustle of modernity, with quiet parks and glimpses into the modern courtyard space of apartment complexes.

In Hangzhou, it is grimy and urban, where the insides of shops are more attractive than walking on the street, unless you slip into the peacefulness of the Xi Hu Lake parks and gardens.

In Shenzhen, it's a stroll in the suburbs with a little more care because thievery is more common. Expensive earrings and jewellery are for private display at events, not for wearing in public where they can be snatched. The CBD and the new high-tech areas in Nan Hai are different, with their modern Asian affluence.

Walk the Bell Tower or the remnant of the city wall in Xi'an and it's a mix of history and ancient stonework peppered with the smell of roasting mutton and cumin. The university areas have shady lanes crowded with street vendors and bicycles. These are ancient streets with ancient trees and history under every footstep, unless you travel to the new suburbs of stark apartments and bleak clinical industrialism. If you are lucky, you may have the opportunity to walk amongst the orchards on the loess plains on the way to the terracotta warriors, or glimpse the cool homes carved from the loess escarpments that border some of the fields.

It's a long walk from a hotel lobby, to cheap food, to the loess plains of Xi'an. Every city has a character and feel that is different from its tourist face. Walking by yourself gives you the opportunity to explore these alternatives while still clutching a safe return ticket to your hotel.

## CHINA BITE

You do not have to stay in the hotel prison. Take your hotel address card and take a risk strolling through local shopping centres to get a better understanding of the people and the country.

# Chapter 28

# EATING WITH YOUR MISTAKES

Walking around is the first step to better engagement with the Chinese environment. Eating outside of the hotel and high-class restaurants is a much more exciting and rewarding challenge. Eating in China is fun, but the more adventurous you become, the more mistakes you will make. There will be times when you want a simple meal by yourself, or perhaps with a European friend who also does not speak Chinese. Take the plunge and try new smaller restaurants. A crowded restaurant is a good choice because the food will usually be good quality and fresh. So many customers are not usually wrong, and high turnover means food is freshly prepared. You will make mistakes, so here are some tips for a recovery that gives you face and also gives face to the restaurant.

There are plenty of restaurant choices beyond the limited ranges of Western adjusted Chinese regional cooking offered in your home country. Don't limit yourself to cuisines you already know. The adventure starts with different styles of food in different restaurants. At worst you may be served with something you find unpleasant.

A vegetarian meal at a Buddhist restaurant comes with a wonderful array of choices. The meal starts with a sushi style rollup of carrots, lettuce, tomatoes. The morning glory is cooked beautifully, just crisp, in a tangy sauce. Fried tofu and peanuts coated in a pepper/chilli-based crunchy covering, the whole dish resplendent with dried red chillies or mushroom stuffed jiaozi. Enjoy a cold dish of lotus roots, lotus buds, water chestnuts, black fungus, green peas and kale. Finish the meal with a pitcher of pumpkin soup.

Xinjiang-style restaurants serve mutton spiced with cumin and chili powder. Breakfast is a simple five spice and chilli *gan* tofu, or *dou hua* 豆花 — bean curd and *you tiao* 油条 — deep fried bread sticks.

Other restaurants offer Harbin-style *jiaozi* — pork, celeriac, spring onion, and other vegetables, all freshly cooked and bundled into fresh jiaozi pastry. They are served with a simple sauce mixture of soy sauce, black vinegar, sesame oil, chilli paste/oil and some crushed garlic. Or maybe try Hangzhou-style roast goose and goose cooked in a hotpot soup with sponge-like bamboo fungus. It's a lot of meat counterbalanced by sweet potatoes, radish, lettuce, celeriac and other vegetables in the hot pot.

You may be the only foreigner in the restaurant so expect some confusion as the wait staff decide amongst themselves who is going to serve you. It may be a young girl from the countryside with rudimentary English, or it may be the manager who may cheerfully greet you with "Good Morning" at nine in the evening. Give them a smile and remember when you were learning and said *zao an* 早安 (Good morning) when you really meant *wan shang hao* 晚上好 (Good evening).

You will be under close observation, just out of curiosity. Some people find this uncomfortable. At times the chef may come to the kitchen door and watch while you eat the meal that he has prepared for you. If you find this prospect intimidating then it may be best to sit with your back facing the kitchen door. Even when you have a menu with pictures, it is possible to make some significant mistakes, which may include:

- Finding that the dish you have ordered looks nothing like the picture.
- Discovering that the dish is much, much larger than the dish in the picture.
- Receiving a dish that is exactly the same as the picture, but with a taste different from what you imagined.
- Accidentally ordering a small banquet designed for three people. The wait staff just assumed all Westerners have a large appetite so they said nothing. When the staff get together and smother their giggles behind their hands it is usually a sign you have over-ordered.

- Being served a dish that turns out to be far less appetising than you imagined.

These are all normal mistakes. Sometimes the mistakes are edible, but at other times they are not. Here are several methods to recover from these errors that will give you face and save face for the restaurant.

First, sample a small part of every dish you have ordered.

If it is really unpalatable, then play with your food for a few minutes until all the dishes you ordered have arrived. Then scrabble for your hand phone. Answer the non-existent call, and look concerned. Look at your watch, and explain you are in the middle of a meal. Remember, somebody in the restaurant may understand English, so the conversation needs to be genuine even if the call is non-existent. Wave for staff to come to your table and ask for the bill — *mai dan* 买单 and for the food to be put in a takeaway bag — *da bao* 打包.

If the food is delicious, but simply too much to eat, then just ask for the bill. The usual hand scribbling in the air is a universal sign, otherwise, as mentioned, *mai dan* is the correct call for the bill. In smaller restaurants, there will be an 'off bill' charge for disposable chopsticks and napkins, usually 2 yuan.

All restaurants are equipped to handle *da bao* requests, from the smallest to the largest. It's a common request, so it will not cause offence. Asking for *da bao* for even relatively little leftovers is a face-saving request.

When he hears this, the chef who has been standing by the kitchen door watching you eat, the wait staff, and other diners will all be pleased you like the food enough to take it away. You give them face, and also give yourself face. What you do with your leftovers is a matter between you and your conscience. If you decide to throw it away, then please be discreet. China is a country where food is respected, and also a country where many people do not have enough to eat.

Moving on to another common mistake that Westerners make when dining in China. Tourist groups in Beijing restaurants often ask for individual menus. They are confused and surprised when only a single menu is offered. On their end, restaurant staff are similarly surprised by a request for separate menus and confused when each person gives an individual order.

Food and the appreciation and sharing of food is central to Chinese socialising. Nothing so clearly distinguishes Western and Chinese habits than the approach to ordering and eating food. Western habits encourage individualism. From Thomas Paine and John Locke onwards, the concepts of liberal individualism have been promoted as the ideal solution. It has a long history and it is summarised simply by the way we eat from individual plates, with complete individual meals. In a restaurant, we order meals individually. Each diner is given a menu and dishes are not meant for sharing. Only in the West will chefs talk of 'plating up' a meal.

The Chinese tradition of eating is based upon sharing. The sharing starts with the menu. A table of up to 8 or 10 people will be given a single menu. It is expected that one or perhaps two people, will make the menu selections for the entire table. In a formal situation, this is a complex task requiring a lot of discussion and thought. The waiter expects one person to do all the ordering.

At a formal banquet, the ordering is usually prearranged. It is not from a set menu. The cost, variety and type of dishes is carefully considered and selected to match the status of the guests at the banquet. As a guest you are expected to sample a bit of everything.

The same rules apply at a smaller gathering with 3 or 4 people. This is often a more vigorous discussion as people consider, select or reject choices. Even a small restaurant will offer a menu with 100 plus choices. It can be lots of fun choosing a meal based on the pictures, or taking literal 'pot luck' or more accurately 'menu luck' when the menu is in Chinese.

Before going into a restaurant, ask to look at the menu. Using your hands to go through the motions of opening a book is usually enough to get a menu delivered. You can ask *gei wo cai dan* 给 我 菜 单 give me the menu. If the menu has pictures then it is easy to order just by pointing. If the menu does not have pictures then it is probably wiser to move to another restaurant.

All dishes are meant to be shared amongst many people. The servings are usually small enough for a few mouthfuls of sampling. Selecting food is a joint social event. Asking for a second personal menu suggests something may be wrong with the service.

However, be careful in restaurants with strong Hong Kong antecedents, or a strong Western bias, such as those in Western hotel chains. Here the portion size is larger so a few dishes can quickly turn out to be too much.

In the more local restaurants, the portion size is small, and the order of serving can be disquieting. Chinese restaurants in the West serve wanton dumplings and soup as appetisers, and rice follows as the next course. In China the meal usually starts with cold dishes. This may be followed with meat, bean curd tofu, and vegetable dishes. All forms of carbohydrates and soups are usually served towards the end of the meal. Dumplings, wantons, *jiaozi* are last, just before the rice. The final course is fresh fruit which is often delivered without the need to order it.

In an ordinary restaurant, the interval between courses will be short. The cold dishes are quickly followed by the next hot dish. Because the portions are small, each is finished before the next course arrives.

Eating in China is very enjoyable if you remember the key question. It is not "What am I going to have?" but "What will we order?". A single menu unites a table and turns a meal into a genuine opportunity to develop friendship. Test out some of the less formal restaurants and as your business relationships grow, you may decide to surprise your Chinese colleagues by taking them to something less formal and more local than the restaurants they have chosen for you.

## CHINA BUSINESS BITE

Step outside the business restaurant and try more local options. It's a great way to engage with people and add depth to your China experience.

# Chapter 29

# CHINA — CHANGE WITHOUT CHANGE

Change has so many contradictions in China. Underneath the change many things do not change and we make a mistake if we take the veneer of modernity at face value. There are strong foundations and traditions of behaviour which must be respected. These people-to-people behaviours take us beyond business but they also cement business.

The interaction of the old and the new, of change and stability came together yet again for me at a meal in the Beijing palace built for the younger son of the last Empress of China, Cixi, or the Empress Dowager as we know her. The original rooms have been turned into private dining rooms. It was a bitter cold Beijing night, and the heavy silken drapes were not enough to keep the cold out. The original under-floor heating system had ceased operation a century ago. Instead the room was heated with a freestanding gas heater made in Korea.

When I was growing up, I remember lighting the kerosene lamps in the evenings to provide light in the farmhouse, and I am not that old. I have worked in many areas where every night you had to start up the generator if you wanted light. Telephones came soon after electricity, and they were a two-piece instrument with a separate speaker and earpiece.

I repeat, I am not that old, but the changes I have seen are, in some ways, beyond imagination. My parents' generation rode horses to school, then later caught a school bus, and even later, owned fuel-efficient cars. The 12-kilometre trip to town was over unsealed and difficult roads and not to be taken on a whim. Today, I think nothing of jumping on a multi thousand kilometre flight to Singapore or Beijing.

Life is measurably different.

And life in China is measurably different but across a much smaller time frame. Chinese people of my generation have seen much greater change than I have seen. They have seen this change compressed in time.

This is not generational change. It is inter-generational change and it buzzes through the changing skylines of Shanghai, Beijing, Chongqing and numerous other second tier cities. It also buzzes through the country side with increasing rapidity. Listen not too carefully and you hear the rush towards the full benefits of the 21st century. Listen carefully and you hear the stresses imposed on centuries and generations of old thinking as it adapts to new ways and pressures.

This is innovation, economic expansion, creativity and an entire nation with higher aspirations for themselves and their children. Think the US economic expansion in the late 19th and early 20th century. Our challenge is to equip ourselves to participate in this growth as partners.

The pace of change and progress in China has been spurred by the refocusing on domestic demand as a result of the decline in export demand. China aspires to produce higher quality and valued added goods. Nobody aspires to be the bottom of the pile.

I was reminded again of the nature of this progress while looking at the outfitting of my friend's new apartments in Xi'an. One of the astounding features was the high penetration of foreign produced goods. Light fittings from Japan, appliances from Korea, bathroom fittings from Germany.

The meal in the converted Beijing palace signalled the end of a successful meeting. I accepted the invitation to *san bu* 散步 (stroll) after the dinner. We drifted into Tiananmen Square, walking down the dimly lit side streets. My Chinese colleague slipped his arm around my shoulder. I put my arm around his shoulder and we walked together as he told me of his experience of Tiananmen and pointed out where he had been when a bullet tore through his trousers.

In China, holding hands and walking arm-in-arm with people of the same sex is a sign of closeness amongst friends. It is common to see this amongst Chinese people, and less common to see this between Chinese and *wai guo ren* 外国人 foreigners. You will often see girls and women holding hands as they walk along the street, or shopping together. This tells everyone they are the best of friends. This is socially acceptable.

It is also socially acceptable for men to wrap arms around each other's shoulders in public places. They may be walking down the street, strolling in a public park, or having a meal together. This body contact amongst men is a signal of strong friendship and trust.

It is becoming increasingly common to see young couples holding hands in the street and in public places, particularly in larger cities such as Beijing, Shanghai, Shenzhen and Guangzhou. When you move away from these cities, even in larger cities like Dalian, Nanjing and Xi'an, this public hand holding is less common. This body contact between men and women is a habit of young people.

Older people are often deeply conservative when it comes to public body contact between men and women in the workplace or in public. In public, and in the workplace, many people would prefer to limit body contact to shaking hands with members of the opposite sex. It is often good practice to avoid even this unless it is initiated by your Chinese counterpart. A simple nod of your head in acknowledgement when introduced is sufficient.

The Western habit of giving a kiss on the cheek when introduced to a female business counterpart is a definite mistake in a business situation. It should not be attempted as it will cause deep embarrassment to all concerned. You cannot afford to start a meeting by instantly creating resentment and embarrassment.

Many older people regard undoing the top button on a shirt as a sign of impropriety. Do this simply because the day is hot and you may be sending a signal you would prefer to avoid. On the other hand, on hot days, Chinese men routinely roll up their T-shirt to expose their midriff. This is quite acceptable, though not recommended for Caucasians.

Modern as China is, the ties with the past remain strong. Westerners discount these at their peril.

Ask any American what happened in 1861 and they will quickly tell you it was the start of the Civil War. They may well mention the battle of Bull Run. This is a core part of the American education curriculum. Ask what significant event happened two years earlier in 1860 and they would probably be unable to tell you.

Ask any Chinese about 1860 and they will rapidly tell you this is the end of the Second Opium War. They will mention the surrender of Hong Kong to the British and the sacking of Yuan Ming Yuan, the old Summer Palace in 1860. Ask what significant event happened two years later in 1861 and they would also probably be unable to tell you.

For both groups, these 160-year-old historical incidents provide important touch points to today's events. Their influence on today's politics cannot be discounted because it runs deep within the cultural fabric of the nation. For the United States, this was seen in the 2020 Black Lives Matter demonstrations that sought a resolution to issues that have remained unresolved since the 1861 American Civil War. The toppling of statues of pro-slavery confederate generals, and the proposal to cut the confederate flag from the Mississippi state flag underlines the power of this historical narrative.

Whether one agrees or disagree, the impact of this American historical legacy is not disputed nor disparaged. Foreign observers may shake their head in bewilderment, but they do not seek to intervene in this domestic fracas with its large-scale demonstrations, the over-the-top police responses and the incitement to violence coming from some US leaders.

For China, the influence of events from the same 1860 historical period are seen in the determination to avoid a repeat of the One Hundred Years of Humiliation. This determination manifests itself in politics and in a newfound confidence about China's place in the global order.

Just as stone statues are a physical reminder of the American Civil War, two tangible examples provide Chinese people with similar reminders every day. The first is Hong Kong which was taken by the British as booty for the Second Opium War in 1860. The second is

Taiwan which was snatched in the last rush of the imperial carve-up of China by the Japanese in 1895.

The legacy of imperialist interference in the domestic policies of China means that foreign observers feel they have the right to intervene in the handling of these issues. Whilst Western countries are content to observe the chaotic legacy of the 1861 civil war in the United States, they do not protest when the United States and the United Kingdom want to interfere with the domestic politics of China that has its roots in the same historical period.

These historical forces flow equally strongly in both societies but receive the global tick of legitimacy in only one. Any mention of the Opium Wars or of the Century of Humiliation is greeted with eye-rolling in the Western media. The subtext is clear — that's in the past so get over it. This failure to understand how history impacts on the present distorts Western understanding of China and, if you allow it, your ability to do business in China.

One historical event in the United States caused deep and ongoing divisions. The other historical event in China became a cause of enduring unity. The impact of both events should not be underestimated or ridiculed when assessing business approaches.

The physical change in the Chinese landscape is rapid. Changes in behaviour and attitudes is a slower process. Modernity continues to have well-entrenched conservative Chinese characteristics.

## CHINA BUSINESS BITES

Don't be fooled by modern exteriors. Old habits and customs continue to exert strong influence. Business is built on relationships so be aware of the behaviours which indicate strengthening friendships. Be respectful of conservative attitudes.

# Chapter 30

# GETTING AROUND

WeChat and WePay have dramatically changed the landscape when it comes to payment for taxis, snacks and souvenirs. Unfortunately, most Western visitors do not have access to WePay so they are stuck with cash.

Walk-around cash delivers most value because it pays for the taxi, the meals in smaller restaurants where credit cards are not an option. These bites cover the basics of cash, taxis and airline travel inside China.

Getting extra cash in foreign locations is not always a seamless activity. Cities in China have a good network of ATMS. They are located in shopping malls, hotel lobbies and a variety of sometimes quite unexpected positions. Not only are they common, but they are also bilingual.

Your Visa card can be used in the same way as in your home country. Insert the card into the ATM and you are given a choice of English menu or Chinese menu. Withdrawals, or cash advances are handled in the same way as they are at home. Many ATMS have a physical security protection device over the keypad to prevent the card from being skimmed so using the ATM is quite safe. It is a good idea to use an ATM in a crowded location as this is generally safer.

In larger cites it is easy to use your Visa card. Many places will accept it. Generally, I carry about 1,200 RMB as walk-around cash. It is easy to have this changed into RMB in Singapore so you have taxi cash when you land in Beijing or Shanghai. Beijing Airport to Tiananmen Square is less than 200 RMB. Pudong airport to the Bund in Shanghai is less than 150 RMB.

If you prefer to carry dollar cash and convert it at the hotel desk, or a bank, then you need to be aware of two things.

First, your dollar notes must be perfect. No creases, folded corners, tears or holes. Make sure no one has used the notes as a writing pad to jot down messages. Notes damaged in any way will not be accepted. It's a problem if you are relying on this cash for converting to RMB. Second, all money changing will require your passport. The hotel desk will need this to complete the transaction details.

You can be more adventurous and change money at the bank. Again, you will need your passport to complete the transaction.

Like all banks, Chinese banks have queues, but rather than stand in line, customers sit in the comfortable chairs. When you enter the bank there is a ticket machine with a touch screen. The service you need is usually found by pressing the button in the upper left-hand corner. Many banks are now using bilingual screens. There are staff who will assist you to press the correct button. It may take a few seconds for a staff member with a smattering of English to be located to assist you. The machine issues you with a numbered ticket. Take it, then sit down and relax.

Your ticket number will be called out over the PA system. It's a good way to practise your understanding of numbers in Chinese. The numbers are read separately, so 208 is read out as *er, ling, ba*. If listening for your number is too complicated, then you can always cheat by watching the scrolling electronic screen above the line of tellers. It will flash the number being served and the correct counter number. Some banks also provide bilingual PA announcements.

Of course, just getting the numbers right is just one step. Next you have to complete the banking transaction. This is a civilised situation, so you sit down at the counter. The teller is behind a glass screen and communication is via a microphone. Slide your passport and dollars under the window. Many tellers will speak some English, but a combination of passport and dollar notes sends the message you would like to change money. You will be asked to sign a transaction slip before your RMB is passed through to you.

On the counter there is a press button device where you can record your comments about the service. The choices are Very good (很好 or

非常好), good (好) or not good (不好). Sometimes these buttons are bilingual. It is polite to press the Very good (很好 or 非常好) and generally this is a genuine feeling. I have found the service much better than many Western banks. I look at the way I am treated in a Chinese bank as a foreigner with limited language skills and compare this with my observations of the way foreigners with limited language skills are treated at my local bank.

Getting money from the ATM with your Visa card is easy. Changing money at the hotel desk is unexciting. Changing money at the bank is more interesting. It's a worthwhile experience even if you only try it once.

Equipped with cash you can try catching your first taxi from the street. Taxi horror stories in foreign places are a legion. I find I have been given the tourist ride rather than the direct route more frequently in different cities in my home country but never in Beijing. I did have a taxi driver who did get lost in Beijing. He turned the meter off and refused to take extra payment when we eventually arrived at the destination. Without exception I have found taxi drivers helpful, honest and pleasant but there are a few useful rules.

1. Never go with a driver who approaches you at the airport. Drivers who approach you are usually *hei che* — illegal and meterless 'black taxis'. Leave the building and head for the taxi queue.
2. If you have to flag down a passing taxi, use the Singapore taxi signal, arm outstretched below head height and hand waving in a 'slow down' motion. Some people call this 'patting the dog'.
3. Some people suggest that if you're staying in an upmarket hotel, then do not go with taxis called by the doorman or waiting in line outside. They claim drivers pay kickbacks to the doormen to allow them to join the line on the forecourt. This may be true, but even if kickbacks are paid it is not a cost to you, and, it's the service you get that counts. In the US you pay the kickback 'tip' to the doorman to get a taxi, and to the taxi driver for accepting you as a passenger! These will be metered taxis and if the driver wants continued support from the hotel, he will make sure you get to your destination without complaints.

4. Take a phone photo of the hotel's business card in Chinese to show to a taxi driver when you want to return to your hotel.

5. Look to see if the taxi supervision card, usually with a photo of the driver and a telephone number, is prominently displayed, as regulations require. If it isn't then it's a black taxi. Choose another taxi.

6. Black taxis are a risk, but at times they are a necessary convenience. Standing in the snow in Shanghai at 6pm in January I found it impossible to flag down a taxi. I eventually caught a black taxi and agreed on the price before getting in. I paid extra in conversation as the driver quizzed me on the meaning of Valentine's Day and how to pronounce it in English.

   Shanghai has many black cabs and they fill a useful gap. Leaving the Shanghai World Expo grounds in 2008, it was impossible to find a taxi, so we started to walk in the general direction of our hotel. Having attended two official dinners, we were well dressed but poorly equipped for the sudden torrential downpour, so we took a black taxi because nothing else was available. We agreed on the price before getting in. The driver had learned his English from American action movies and was keen to practise. He did not know the location of the Pudong Intercontinental hotel, and the paper hotel address card did not help because it had disintegrated in the rain. The rain was so heavy it was difficult to read street signs so even talking to the hotel staff over the phone for directions was not successful.

   What would usually be a 10-minute journey from the hotel to our destination ended up being a 40-minute trip with many false turns. The English-Chinese conversation was an experience well worth the cost of the taxi fare. Giving directions in fractured Chinese as I recognised some landmarks illuminated for a few seconds by lightning flashes added to the experience. This was an unexpected small adventure, although my wife did not have quite the same perspective.

7. Always make sure you hear the meter reset. In Beijing it delivers a recorded greeting in Chinese and English "Welcome to my taxi". Some say that if you don't see the flag pushed down, which shouldn't

happen until you actually move off, then you may end up paying for the time the taxi was in the queue. This is supposed to be a particularly popular scam outside Western hotels. It is difficult to see how this scam works as meters have an automatic flag fall minimum based on distance. In any case, it is demeaning to argue over a few renminbi.

8. If you are by yourself, sit in the back seat. You are a Westerner and this is about face. Where possible give the driver the destination written in Chinese. Ask the concierge to write it for you. It is pointless to pretend to look as if you know where you are going if you don't know. If the driver looks confused, then ring your destination and get them to talk to the driver and give directions. This is less common nowadays with the universal availability of WeChat maps.

9. Pay what's on the meter. Tips are not required. The driver will insist on giving change. Always ask for a receipt — *wo yao fa piao* 我要发票 — as it has the taxi licence plate number and a phone number. If you leave something in a taxi, I am told there's a remarkably high success rate at getting even valuable items back if you call the number on the receipt and provide the details. You'll need the assistance of a Chinese speaker. If you decide to give a tip for exceptional service then do so after the correct payment has been made. I gave a tip to a driver who used back streets to avoid an unexpected extended Beijing traffic jam to get me to the airport in time to catch my flight. She was reluctant to accept because she felt she had just done her job. In Shanghai and Shenzhen, you may find a more mercenary approach to accepting tips.

Taxi drivers are happy to take on longer engagements. A friend and I did a short one-day trip from Hangzhou to Shao Xing just for tourism. The taxi fare and the use of the same taxi and driver for the entire trip came to less than $200. We had used the taxi the previous day on a short trip from the hotel for a business meeting and the driver was courteous and helpful, so we took his WeChat contact details. When we decided to go to Shao Xing, we contacted him because we were confident of his ability.

Tourists are coddled with prebooked flights and fares from the time they leave their home airport to the time they arrive. Business requires more flexibility, particularly with domestic air travel inside China. Arranging a quick trip from Beijing to Shanghai or Xi'an is not a major obstacle. Getting around China often appears difficult, but this is not the case.

Arranging domestic air travel in China is a simple task. Beijing airport runs more domestic flights per day using wide body and jumbo jets than many international airports handle on a daily basis. There are around eight flights every hour from Beijing to Shanghai. Finding flight availability is usually not a problem.

The days of using a hotel airline booking service or travel agency are long gone. CTrip or QuNar online travel services allow for rapid and efficient online bookings that can be paid for with an international credit card. I find CTrip the best for Western users. You can use these services on a casual basis, but it is even more efficient if you pre-register all the relevant details including passport numbers and card details.

You will need your passport to finalise the booking and when collecting your boarding pass. It's a domestic flight, but your passport fills the same function as an identity card.

Book a one-way ticket. The same principles apply for the return flight. It is cheaper to book a few days ahead than it is to get a return ticket. This also gives you flexibility as business arrangements change. Tickets are electronic and issued on the spot and emailed to your nominated address or WeChat account.

A bit of flexibility can reap significant savings. I find it useful to just book an international flight from my home to Beijing or Shanghai. As business develops, I book internal Chinese domestic flights as necessary. It is much cheaper, and it gives me flexibility in reacting to developing opportunities.

In China, airline seats are allocated from the front to the back. This means the last two back rows of seats are often empty. If you feel cramped for space, or want to have a nap on the flight, then simply go to the last two back rows and sit there when you board the plane. Odds are you will have three seats to yourself. If the seats have been allocated you simply plead ignorance and return to your ticketed seat. No offence will be taken as this is a common practice. Do not wait until the plane has taken off to change seats. Someone will have beaten you to it.

All Chinese airports use automated check-in terminals. In most cases you can use your passport in place of the Chinese identity card. Terminals are bilingual and they speed up the check-in process.

Getting around China is easier than you may imagine. You do not need to work with organised tour groups and their schedules. Catching a taxi to even a well-known tourist area gives you flexibility to work around changes in business schedules. Moving outside the well-known Western tourist destinations gives you a very different perspective of people.

## CHINA BUSINESS BITE

You can step away from the guided tour and mingle with people on your own terms and schedules. Take the opportunity to use readily available taxis to explore in your own time. Getting there and back requires pre-planning, but getting around China can be much more flexible.

# Chapter 31

# WHERE THE CHINESE GO

Western tourists go to China to see the Great Wall, the Forbidden City, the Temple of Heaven and the terracotta warriors in Xi'an. The choices many Chinese tourists make when they tour China are often very different and reflect a profound difference in cultural backgrounds. The Chinese tourists' list will feature museums, temples, more museums, mountains and perhaps a gaudy theme park or two. It's the museums that provide the insights into Chinese culture and thinking that in turn broadens your understanding of China and its people.

These brief travel notes are more personal and reflect observations of tourist destinations favoured by my Chinese friends. Westerners are few and far between. These notes are a bite designed to reflect the alternatives to what we see in Western tour groups. It is where the Chinese go.

In Chengdu we have time to fit in a visit to the garden museum home of the Du Fu Thatched Cottage Museum. This is the former, and now reconstructed, residence of the Tang Dynasty poet, Du Fu 杜甫. These are very extensive gardens with stands of bamboo that thrive in the colder mountain air.

The Du Fu Thatched Cottage Museum hides a complex of gardens with tall bamboo, landscaped scenery, wonderful bonsai landscapes with Guilin limestone karst rocks soaring into the mist, running streams, and small pavilions. The landscape and environment that Dufu mentions in his poems is drawn from the reality of this Chengdu location.

Later on, we have time to visit the Wuhou Temple, and nearby Jinli street. This temple was built in 223 AD. It is an essential part of the Romance of the Three Kingdoms. It commemorates the oath of the peach garden. Liu Bei, Guan Yu and Zhang Fei, who although bearing different family names, bound themselves as sworn brothers in a ceremony amid the peach blossom trees. This type of strong relationship amongst friends is central to much of Chinese thinking.

Not surprisingly, in the temple visits and the Dufu area I find I am the only Westerner. I do not see another foreign face.

The Wuhou Temple complex includes a shop filled with black silky buried wood. On the Chengdu plain there are buried trees 3,000 years or more old. It's a thick, dark, heavy grained wood. The wood is not petrified, but deeply preserved. It is used for smooth black silky carvings and wooden objects. There are lots of imitations, but once you feel the genuine wood you can tell the difference. It has a unique silky smoothness and density. These trees are uncovered during the frequent earthquakes.

Jinli street just outside the temple is crowded and includes many good local eating places. This is the Chinese tourist version of traditional China in Chengdu. Afterwards, we stop briefly at *kuan zhai xiang zi* 宽窄巷子. It's a mix of Shanghai's Xintiandi and Beijing's 798 art area. *Kuan zhai xiang zi* is an old neighbourhood that got a thorough facelift, so it is now a trendy pedestrian alley fusing beautifully restored traditional architecture with modern and well-appointed restaurants, teahouses, cafes, restaurants and shops. This has a mix of up-market tourism, nightclubs, and Chinese up-scale dining that makes you feel as if you are in Hong Kong. It's the tourist version of Chengdu and it has more foreigners.

In Hangzhou for business, we decide to visit the small town of Shao Xing 绍兴. We hire a taxi to take us there, it is about 50 km from the city. We visit the homes of famous revolutionary writers now turned into museums. It is an area with a long literary history and also home to ancient writers. We visit the Shen Yuan 沈园 garden with its memorial to the Southern Song Dynasty poet Lu You 陆游. Sitting on a rock overlooking the gardens it seems natural for visitors to discuss the differences between Song and Tang dynasty poetry structures and the way romantic poems always go badly for the characters involved. Only in China can you get an eager crowd of poetry tourists.

Later on, we go to Lan Ting 兰亭 to visit where Jin Dynasty calligrapher Wang Xi Zhi 王羲之 completed the famous Lan Ting Xu preface 兰亭序 — Preface to the Poems Composed at the Orchid Pavilion. The original is lost but the earliest copy is located in the Palace Museum in Beijing. Numerous later copies hang in Chinese homes and offices throughout China.

The scenery is beautiful, with mountains, streams, bamboo groves and paths. In this area it is common to see stone tables being used as writing desks. Students stand, brush in hand, practising their calligraphy, writing with water on the stones. I have seen this done on concrete paths in parks using giant brushes in Hangzhou and Shanghai but it is the first time I have seen these facilities deliberately provided for recreation. It is an impermanent graffiti table. People cluster around, admiring the calligraphy, or the poetry selection.

Mountain climbing also appeals to many. *Tai Shan* 泰山 mountain in Shandong province is one of the five sacred mountains in China. You can walk from the base, or start the journey part of the way up the mountain by taking a ride in a never-ending procession of buses. We take a taxi to the base of Tai Shan. This is a Chinese mountain so it is *ren shan ren hai* 人山人海 — people mountain people sea — crowded. There is a constant circle of buses picking people up every 5 minutes and taking them to the middle station on the mountain.

This is not a climb in mountain solitude the kind beloved of European soul-seeking individualists. There are no secluded spots of genuine tranquillity. Tai Shan mountain is granite torr thrust layer upon layer, uplifted to vertical and squeezed. The higher you go, the more expensive things become. Everything for sale is manually carried up the mountain.

The porters carry massive loads swinging from bamboo poles on their shoulders. We pause to talk to one porter who is having a rest. There are thick hard calluses on his shoulders.

The mountain is warm, with only an occasional breeze floating up the steep valley.

The mountain is climbed by young and old. It is little children and old pensioners, all caught in the same breathlessness of the climb. It is *yi bu yi bu* 一步一步 — step by step we go, breathing more laboured as we move higher.

Every now and then the clouds swirl up the ravine, lightly caressing our sweating faces before disappearing soundlessly into the foliage. It is refreshing, but not sustaining. We pause at Cloud Street, just below the temples on the summit of the mountain. The clouds swirl upwards, cloaking the street and its vendors in drifts of mist, then baking us in the sharp sunlight.

From Cloud Street we go to the peak of the mountain. This is dominated by temples and the highest is the Daoist temple. The top of the mountain is covered in a snow-white carpet of plum blossoms, and the light scent freshens the air.

In the process I understand one of the reasons why we have come to Tai Shan. My friend's new apartment does not have the best feng shui. A rock from Tai Shan placed in the right location will correct this. The apartment is for her parents, so these measures are important. Taking rocks from Tai Shan is prohibited but thousands of Chinese ignore the regulations. In a millennium, they may succeed in carrying away the mountain, bit by bit.

We walk around the side of the peak, cheek by jowl with precipitous drops, magnificent views and a rock fall between two towering spikes of rock. The fall has been captured and halted, rocks jumbled together to form a bridge, a chasm below. Time is limited so we take the cable car down to the middle station. As backpacks are lowered to the floor of the gondola, I hear the tell-tale clunk of forbidden rocks. We are locked in a rice bubble with seven others, including a young lady who is almost hysterically frightened, clutching her boyfriend who is himself also almost rigid with fear.

It's a parachute fall, the wind whistling through the open grill in the upper edges of the gondola, and then howling as the cable reaches across a chasm. It is beautiful, silent falling with just the muffled sounds of small sobs of fear from one passenger.

Chinese domestic tourism is larger than Chinese international travel. The Chinese travel to Xishuangbanna in Yunnan, remote from both Beijing and Shanghai. They stare over desert wasteland past the Westernmost remnants of the Great Wall in Gansu province after visiting the ancient Buddhist grottos in Dunhuang. Western visitors are almost a curiosity.

When we see Chinese tourists in Western countries, we most often associate them with noisy shopping expeditions and the purchase of cheap souvenirs. We make the assumption that this drives domestic Chinese tourism as well. Whilst there are certainly elements of this, it is unwise to ignore the cultural imperatives which drive significant sections of Chinese tourism. Chinese museums are crowded with Chinese people connecting with a very real and living history, particularly with poetry, philosophers and artists. Europeans who frequent their own museums will have noticed an increase in the number of Chinese tourists. They may be more animated and noisier than we prefer, but their interest in the culture captured in the museum is genuine.

Where the Chinese choose to go and the places they choose to visit in domestic tourism provides deep insights into the Chinese character. If you express an interest in this culture then you are invited into a deeper aspect of business relationships. The calligraphy hanging on the wall of a Chinese office is not a trophy like an artwork hanging in a Western office or foyer. Most often it hangs there as an expression of the owner's genuine cultural appreciation.

## CHINA BUSINESS BITE

If you only go with Western tourists go then you will only see the Western version of China. Take every opportunity to see China as the Chinese see it through a lens of Chinese history.

# Chapter 32

# CHINA CASE STUDY — WORKING WITH TRANSLATORS

Your business survival in China usually depends on somebody else — your translator. The level of dependency will vary from total to almost total, unless you are fortunate enough to be fully fluent in Chinese. Even then, matters of face may demand you limit your fluency to unofficial situations.

Inevitably you will work with translators and interpreters. Learning these co-operation skills is best done in a workshop environment which is a service we provide through www.workingwithChina.com. This chapter is a summary of the essential issues, problems, and some solutions. Every week, I write several thousand words for translation. This includes articles in Shanghai Security News and other Chinese publications. The minefields of misunderstanding even in the written word are extensive. They are even more dangerous in the spoken word and at their worst when you are involved in free flowing translation environments.

Better translation relationships start with the understanding that what is simple for you may be complicated for others in ways you are not aware of. This may include translation format problems and the way the question is formulated. What you say may impact on wider background issues you are not aware of, including cultural sensitivity, political sensitivity and bureaucratic or administrative barriers. In short, you cannot speak as freely or as unthinkingly as you do in your home country because people you are working with do not have your common background of language habits.

There are two key translation decisions. The first is to decide if the translation will be literal and formal, or interpretative. In formal translation, the sentence 'The traveller may have problems adjusting to the local time after arriving on an intercontinental flight' becomes much more complicated. It may read 'The traveller will find their body will not coordinate with local time when they arrive after an intercontinental flight that has passed through several time zones'. These confabulations appear more frequently in written translations, but they are never far from spoken translations.

An interpretative translation may read 'International travellers may suffer jet lag.' It captures the meaning of the sentence without necessarily using the exact words, or the literal translation. An interpreter will give you the translation, the meaning and the intent of the speaker. An excellent interpreter will also give you the speaker's implied meaning.

Our preference lies with interpretative translation unless there are exceptional reasons for using direct or literal translation. This is most often the case in political and official situations or in contract verification.

The second key decision for public speakers is to know if the translation will be consecutive, or simultaneous. Consecutive is when you talk, then the translator talks. For consecutive translation, allow 30% more time. For simultaneous translation allow 10% more time.

The key errors in public speaking presentations where translation is required are:

- Speed — talking too fast and at great length before pausing for the translator to do their work.
- Lack of awareness of translator so you do not know if they are keeping up, understanding, or struggling.
- Repetition errors increase when you speak for too long. The translator must remember what you have said and then repeat it.
- Deviation from prepared texts when giving a keynote speech creates confusion. The translator might simply ignore your comments.

When working in consecutive translation environments, here are the key tips.

- Talk more slowly and in very small sound bites so the translator can listen and translate.
- Develop some agreed signals for when you are speaking too fast, or for when the translator wants you to repeat or rephrase a comment.
- Use definite sentence stops so the translator knows when to start and stop translating.
- Dump the slang — do not use your local language habits or idioms.
- If you have the time, then work with the translator beforehand to make sure they understand your accent. This can just be a simple conversation so the translator can get accustomed to your English, American, Irish or Australian accent.
- Remember this is a partnership. Their voice is your voice. Without their voice you are just making noise.
- If your presentation allows for audience questions, then use interpretative translation for questions and for answers to avoid offence.

Simultaneous translation is much more difficult because there is no translator feedback. Typically, they sit in a small booth at the back of the room and you cannot see them. You must be aware of your speaking speed and language complexity. If you are reading from a set speech this is not a problem because they will have a pre-translated copy to refer to. It does become a problem when you deviate from the set speech, or speak off the cuff.

When working with simultaneous translation environments, there are three key tips.

- Talk more slowly, at about two thirds of your normal speed. Pause a little at the end of each section or paragraph and wait to give the translators time to catch up.
- Stick to the prepared speech if you have one. If you have a strong accent then definitely do not deviate from the prepared speech.

- Arrange for some translator distress signals in advance and watch for signs of distress.
- Talk with translators before the event so they have an opportunity to familiarise themselves with your accent and speaking style.

Language is a complex beast and there are two essential features to avoid in preparing material which will be subject to translation. It is easy enough in a prepared written speech, but these also need to be avoided in an off the cuff speech:

- Complicated sentences in terms of structure. For example: 'With a projected development time frame of 30 years and the market demand for base metals, it is easy to see why the Chinese partners value this project and partnership so highly'. It is much better to say: 'The project will develop over 30 years. The market demand for base metals is strong. This explains why the Chinese partners value this project and partnership'.
- Double or strange negatives. For example: 'It's no surprise China is interested in the project. We are not saying it's impossible they will not be interested.' Try something simpler: 'Of course China is interested in the project, but they might not agree'.

In meetings it is very easy to assume you have agreement and understanding when in fact there is no agreement and no understanding. People on both sides of the table have a tendency to nod their heads in agreement even if they do not fully understand what has been said. It is essential to use a confirmation technique to ensure keys points have been understood. This means rephrasing the question so the original answer is confirmed. The Chinese side will use this method frequently and it drives many Westerners to distraction. Westerners complain "We have already covered this area and agreed", not realising this is the Chinese side reconfirming that their understanding is correct.

Take this simple statement 'The project must be completed by March 15'. And the reply 'Okay. We will do our best'.

Do you have confidence the deadline has been understood? Probably not. Do not ask for the conclusion to be repeated back to you as this implies a loss of face. Reframe the original question in these ways:

- Do you see any problems with the March 15 deadline?
- Are there any other factors or projects which might influence your ability to finish this project on March 15?
- Is the March 15 deadline convenient?
- Do we need to talk to anyone else or organisation about this March 15 deadline?

The answers to these supplementary questions achieve two things. First, the answers confirm the correct understanding of the original question. Second, the different approaches used in the supplementary questions may reveal problems that would not otherwise have been mentioned. This may include the need to get approval from another person, department or authority. By inviting people to let you know the March 15 deadline is inconvenient you give them the opportunity to say this without losing face. If it is inconvenient, then you can be certain the March 15 deadline would not be achieved despite everybody doing their best.

Translation survival rests on three pillars. First you must decide in advance exactly what you want from the translation service. Second it is important to help your translator to help you. Third is to respect their professionalism. Most times if you are misunderstood it is because what you said was unclear. The translator or interpreter is your voice. Without them you are powerless, incomprehensible and stranded.

Translation is most critical in meetings and how you use your translator determines the dynamics of the meeting. Here are 12 tips for every meeting.

1) Look at the speaker, not the translator. The translator is your voice. You are not talking to the translator. You are talking to your counterpart on the other side of the table. Look at them when you talk to them. Look at them when they talk to you. Avoid the

temptation to look at their translator. Often the translator will be an attractive young lady and this provides an unnecessary distraction for many Western men. Keep your mind on your job. Do not flirt with your translator or ask them out. This may cause great embarrassment and offence — something you want to avoid as you remain dependent upon them to accurately translate what you say and any ill-feeling towards you may not be conducive to accuracy.

2) Ignore the translator. You must work with the translator prior to the meeting, but in the formal meeting, the translator is ignored. The translator should sit behind you and to one side. Alternatively, the translator may sit beside you and the host.

3) Pre-arrange cues with your translator to cover a variety of situations. These include when you are speaking too quickly or when you have said something offensive or inappropriate.

4) Speak slowly and in small bites. Avoid using slang or colloquialisms. This feels stilted for a start, but it is easy to get into a rhythm that makes accurate translation easier.

5) Listen carefully to the translation. It may not be exact. Listen carefully for confusion of tenses in terms of time. When in doubt ask for clarification but do so in a way that does not cast doubt upon the translator's ability. It is better to say you didn't hear clearly rather than to say you didn't understand the translation.

6) Use precise language when you talk. Avoid imprecision because this may be translated in a way that implies precision.

7) Don't assume others at the table or in the meeting cannot understand English. They may choose not to reveal this for many reasons. Often it is related to face. They may understand, but lack confidence in their English fluency. A key giveaway is to watch for involuntary smiles when you are speaking and before your comments have been translated. This will tell you who has a good understanding of English. Of course, this cuts both ways. If your understanding of Chinese is okay, but you are not so fluent, then you may also choose not to reveal your language skill. However, avoid the temptation to smile as the Chinese side is speaking and

before the translation is completed. The same applies to starting the polite applause before the translator has signalled the end of the presentation.

8) Some circumstances may require dual translation. You have a translator for English to Chinese and they have a translator for Chinese to English. In this situation it is even more important to remember to work directly with the person you are speaking to.

9) Always give face to their translator because this also gives face to the other people. Do not insist on using your own translator. They can always brief you on any issues or mistranslations later as necessary.

10) Allow for translator to translator discussion and clarification. This will help get the best interpretation and the best result. It avoids confusion.

11) Give face to your translator by showing you respect their work, their skill and the effort required. Respect can be as simple as not talking continuously for three minutes and then expecting a full and accurate translation.

12) Work with the translator because this is a partnership. They are not machines. They are much better than a machine because their translation and interpretation skills will prevent you from making literal mistakes.

## CHINA BUSINESS BITE

It's a complex area which is better explained via a workshop environment working in simulated translation situations with direct feedback. Much better to practise this at home in your office and find the errors than to do it for the first time in Beijing and make the same errors in public. Remember this is a partnership. Their voice is your voice. Without their voice you are just making noise.

# Chapter 33

# COPYCATS GET LEFT BEHIND

There remains a popular idea that China is a nation of copycats with stores full of fake goods created with ideas stolen from others. There is an element of truth, but ironically this copycat mantra is itself copied and repeated ad nauseam from the US President and Fox News commentators down to the man in the street.

This ill-informed concept of China is not only an exercise in ignorance, but more importantly it also blinds us to the vast research and development industry that underpins China's new economy. Chinese telecommunications manufacturer Huawei operates research and development centres in China that dwarf their counterparts in the US.

But it's not just research that poses a challenge. It is the new thinking that goes with the research. Four examples sum up the nature of the competition and the opportunity.

The first is the development of WePay and AliPay. Superficially, these look similar to the American internet payment models like ApplePay. Scratch the surface and the difference is immediately obvious. The US model is based on Apple getting between you and your bank and taking a slice of the action with new fees and commissions. Uber takes the same path.

WePay and AliPay are a completely new model that allows the customer to deal directly with the merchant in a way that makes micro-payments possible. It doesn't rewrite the rules; it creates an entirely new game.

The second example comes from a humble multi-storey car park. In Xi'an I visited the new shopping centre Sai Ge. After a good lunch it was difficult to remember exactly where we had parked the car.

As with all modern car parks, we had passed under an Automatic Number Plate recognition gantry. In the West this is used to issues fines for parking evaders and over-stayers. China takes the next step. They use this information to identify where each car is parked. Enter your registration number at any one of the terminals in the car park and a map showing the exact location of your car is displayed along with the shortest route to it. It took less time to find our car than it did to decide on the lunch restaurant. This is China taking the next step by using data in innovative ways in a service economy.

It's a long way from high tech Sai Ge shopping centre to the third example on the Mongolian grasslands where sheep are still herded by shepherds. An enterprising shepherd developed an app for tracking his sheep. Rather than enduring the summer heat or the winter cold outside watching his sheep, he is able to track his sheep, know where they are located and know the weather conditions in that location from the comfort of his home. It saves time and effort and improves shep-herding efficiency.

The next step? This tracking information is the first step in the fresh food logistics chain. In the supermarkets in Beijing you can track your cut of mutton back to the grassland where the sheep was born. You can know how much weight it gained, what grass it ate, the water it drank and its health. Not all of us want to do this, but this tracking is used to guarantee quality and protect against fake substitution.

The fourth example comes from married life. Singles day — 11th November — and China's Valentine's Day — *Qixi* — provide some insights into the changing nature of married, and unmarried life in China.

Singles Day is a modern commercial construct designed to sell products. It's called Singles Day, not because it is aimed at unmarried people, but because the four ones in the date — 11/11 — are all 'singles'. It is clever marketing.

*Qixi* or *Qiqiao* Festival, has a longer tradition dating back to the Han dynasty. Like many traditions, it has become commercialised. The day comes from a traditional love story between Zhinu, a weaver girl and Niulang, a cowherd. Their love was forbidden so they were banished to opposite sides of the Silver River. Once a year, on the 7th day of the 7th lunar month, a flock of magpies would form a bridge to reunite the lovers for one day.

Now, once a year, social media, TV and radio is swamped by advertising and online deals that range from the truly romantic to those with a high cringe factor. This wave of potential marital bliss obscures some significant changes in Chinese society. Shanghai marketing research firm, *China Skinny*, has put some figures around these changes.

The number of Chinese adults living alone has grown 16% since 2012 to reach around 77 million. Singles are mainly found in tier 1 cities. The average age of women in Shanghai when they first marry is 30 years. This is up from an average age of 27 in 2011. This average hides the fact that there are many more women over 30 getting married for the first time and this is changing the concept of 'leftover women' — a term used to describe unmarried women who are past a certain age.

It also has a significant impact on the consumer preferences of the older unmarried women. They are less likely to be overwhelmed by the latest cute heart-shaped handbag or the saccharine advertising and fluffy stuffed toys that appeal more directly to those in their mid-twenties.

In universities — where many Chinese people traditionally meet their spouses — 70% remain single after graduation. Whilst nagging parents remain a constant feature of post-university match-making, there is a rise of more pleasant web-based alternatives.

The after-marriage market is expanding as couples are twice as likely to get divorced than they were a decade ago. The "Never more ready to fall in love again" campaign in Western markets directed at older clients and divorcees has, as yet, no equivalent in China. It's a market niche waiting to be filled.

The single audience is increasingly well catered for. Hot pot chain Haidilao offers solo diners a choice of large, cuddly soft toys to join them for dinner to help them feel less lonely. Japanese chain Muji introduced smaller rice cookers, ovens and kettles aimed at Chinese singles. Food and beverage brands are increasingly offering single-serve formats for dinner and other meals. The rapid rise of food delivery has been largely driven by singles with 65% of food delivery orders on Meituan-Dianping going to singles.

It is China's ability, not just to innovate, but then take the next step beyond innovation and adapt that really challenges our business-as-usual approach. That's where the challenges to our business models are found, and also where future opportunities are located. Copycats and lazy cats get left behind.

## CHINA BUSINESS BITE

The Chinese consumer of your Western services is smart, sophisticated, and wedded to e-commerce. Contrary to political propaganda, the Chinese do not rely on copy-technology for success.

# Chapter 34

# GETTING RICH WITH FRIENDS

China has been a rich source of myths and curiosities since Marco Polo put down his embroidered recollections on paper. Many of his claims seem unsophisticated to modern readers but we are not immune to some equally unsophisticated beliefs about China today. Several of these are modern myths and while some are relatively harmless misconceptions, others are based squarely on anti-Chinese sentiment and designed as money making or money taking opportunities. In this section we look at a very small selection of these myths and how they impede our ability to do business.

China is also home to many clichés which often rest on a kernel of truth. Clichés overstate the truth and at times assume almost mythical status. The concept of *guanxi* is both a cliché and a myth. It's a valuable concept but it creates confusion when we think about how to do business in China.

How do you do business in or with China? If you are a large multinational company there is a clearly defined path. If you are a small to medium enterprise (SME) the task is more difficult. The same problems apply from the Chinese side. The SINOPECs of the China business landscape have a well-defined path for investment and business, but the smaller companies find it more difficult.

Enter the *guanxi* cliché. For China business the phrase "I've got a friend" takes on a whole new meaning. When we say "I have a friend who can help" in a Western business context, it can be taken as a casual statement, or it may be seen as somehow touching on the dishonest. We tend to treat the claim with greater suspicion if the 'friend' is overseas.

This is unfortunate because this relationship lies at the very heart of small business engagement with China. I chatted recently with a Australian-based steel importer. He imports steel from Guangzhou. Although he is an Australian-born Chinese, he speaks no Chinese at all. However, he has a friend in Hong Kong who assists him with contract and specification negotiations. This friendship opened up the potential for doing business with China.

Friendships are the foundation of Chinese business. It is a cliché, but it is an inescapable reality. It applies at the small end of town and also at the big end of town. Andrew Forrest, CEO of Fortescue Metals drew on personal friendships to secure supplies of protective COVID masks from China for the Australian Government, and he then successfully blocked attempts by US Government buyers to outbid for the masks before the loaded airplane took off. These friendships apply to Westerners doing business in China and for China companies doing business in the West. In China business, it pays to choose your friends very carefully.

In Shanghai and Beijing, whilst participating in discussions with MOFCOM (Ministry of Finance and Commerce) and the China Import Export Bank, I hear this concept of business with friends raised frequently. Chinese businesses first look to friends or colleagues in America, or France or Australia for business advice and assistance. This has some significant drawbacks, particularly as investment deals become larger and more complex. However, it underlines the degree to which much China-related business starts with friends and colleagues and their connections.

My own work in China started with 'friends' who were working in the same industry area. Without these introductions and support, the business I have in China would never have grown. The nature of business in China means friendship plays a more important role than it does in the Western environment. For SMEs, business is still possible without the help of friends, but business is often more successful with the support from a friend who can help.

And this begs a question. How do you establish these friendship networks? Some people have a natural advantage. They may be part of, or involved in, the expat Chinese community. Other opportunities may emerge through engagement with Chinese companies and staff.

However, one of the most significant ways of tapping into these networks is through the activity of the China Business Councils based in your home country. As your business expands in China you may want to be involved in the business chambers based in China. Home country business groups include the Australia China Business Council, the Singapore Chinese Chamber of Commerce and the US China Business Association. These business council events bring together people who have experience working in and with China. They have networks of friends who can help, and some of their friends may be able to assist you. Typically, membership is drawn from a wide cross section of the business community. The lessons learned by the large companies are still useful for smaller companies.

Multinational organisations such as the Silk Road Chambers of International Commerce also have an important role to play through the informal networks that grow around forums, trade shows and conference events they sponsor.

The path to China is already well trodden. The pitfalls and problems are well known so there is no need for those first starting out to repeat the mistakes made by others. The cost of business council membership is recouped by just one deal that proceeds smoothly, or by one expensive problem avoided because the business council was able to introduce you to 'a friend who can help'.

Nevertheless, as Time Clissold in his book *MR CHINA* highlights, there is also a downside of the 'I've got a friend' approach. Not all friends are created equal. Just as genuine Chinese businesses will take time to evaluate your sincerity and trustfulness, so too should you take the time to do the same. If you intend to share the same bed then it is best to either have the same dreams, or at the very least, dreams which are compatible.

The idea that to get rich is glorious is both a cliché and a myth in thinking about China. There is no denying the ambition to improve personal living standards. There is no denying the drive to make the life of the next generation better than conditions enjoyed by the current generation. It's a path to a moderately prosperous lifestyle. The suggestion that this means anything is acceptable in the pursuit of wealth is misplaced because it fails to understand the way this growth is managed so that it is compatible with broader Chinese political strategies.

Images of Deng Xiaoping, Soviet leader Brezhnev and the ancient Korean leader Kim Il-sung still influence the way many people see China's political leadership. They associate leaders of non-democratic countries with old men, ossified thinking and decision making that is out of touch with the current decade.

This image has been incorrect for some time, with China's leadership at all levels becoming increasingly younger and more broadly educated. This youth is in marked contrast to the leadership in Western democracies where the age of decision makers, on average, is older than in China. The difference is important because it leaves Chinese leadership more open to new ideas and innovative solutions.

This may seem an oxymoron when talking of China which remains dominated by an overriding political philosophy, despite its recasting as socialism with Chinese characteristics. However, the emergence of China as an economic powerhouse rests on radical changes in leadership. Deng Xiaoping is reputed to have said: "To get rich is glorious" and this is taken as evidence of Western envy and greed and an inevitable move to Western capitalism.

What Deng Xiaoping actually said is: "Let some people get rich first. Poverty is not socialism". It's a subtle difference and signalled a change in thinking at a structural level. It underlines the importance of a more careful understanding of the nuances of change and policy development in China.

Policy formulation in Western democracies is driven by popular public criticism and demand, and also by vested interests which retain full-time lobbyists in the nations' capitals. The task of the politician is to balance these robust public policy debates. Academics are often derided, although tame experts and specially commissioned reports are dragged out when necessary.

Public policy formulation in China is an entirely different process. We know this, but we have mythical images of a secretive politburo meeting to develop and decide policy. This is not an accurate picture. China relies on a much broader range of informed public research to develop public policy.

These are what we call 'think tanks' in the West. Their task is to consider a very wide range of public policy issues, solutions and potential policy recommendations. In the West, think tanks are privately funded and small with personnel numbers under 1,000. In China they are publicly funded, very large, and an integral part of public policy debate. Just one of the dozen or so think tanks in Beijing alone, the Chinese Academy of Social Sciences, has fifty research centres covering 260 disciplines with 4,000 full time researchers. The Communist Party Executive Leadership Program based in Pudong is deigned to provide executive and management training for all levels of government. It draws on the world's best practices in a rigorous training program and ongoing professional management education for leaders and officials.

We debate on the streets and increasingly through social media, with equal weight given to the most informed and the least informed participants. The public policy debate in China is a clash of informed ideas, supported by extensive research. We may prefer the noisy open democracy model, but this misses the point in identifying the drivers of China's policymaking.

China favours the idea of an intellectual meritocracy in establishing public policy rather than policy as the product of majority rule or social media hysteria. This is consistent with the Confucian tradition. The British adopted the civil service entry examinations from China to replace the patronage system. China is a keen observer of Singapore which adopted the rule of law without the American style of democracy. Singapore has a thriving economy and provides an alternative model to the democracy of mob rule promoted by the US as the exclusive road to economic success.

## Corruption

Corruption is a sensitive topic in every country but it's a mistake to think corruption is limited to China. There is always corruption and if you go looking for it you will find it. Corruption may come looking for you but what you do about it is an ethical and moral choice you have to make. However, just because it involves a way of doing business that is not familiar to you, it does not mean it is corrupt. Corruption takes many different forms. Some is overt and easily recognised. Other forms are less obvious and they quickly fade into the same grey areas occupied by the billion-dollar lobbyist industry in the US.

You do not have to look as far as China to find corruption on a large scale. There is headline corruption everywhere: including the manipulation of LIBOR interest rates by UK banks during the Global Financial Crisis; the sale of unsafe derivative instruments or CDOs as investment grade securities which led to the collapse of the entire Western banking system; the Bernie Madoff Ponzi scheme; the payments of millions of dollars to Saddam Hussein associates by the Australian Wheat Board and the allegations of payment of secret inflated commissions by agencies of the Australian Reserve Bank note printing arm Securency to gain bank note printing contracts.

In Iraq, large non-tender contracts were awarded by American government officials who had previously been in board positions on the companies that were awarded the contracts. This close relationship between business and government is not so much different to the relationship between government and state-owned enterprises in China. The secret company-specific taxpayer handouts to automobile companies have been described as the insidious corruption of our important public institutions.

Our objective is to get you thinking about the concept. Here are examples of some business practices. Read through them and decide if you think they fall into the category of corruption.

- Extra payment for special service.
- Asked to pay for 'special' service but service not delivered.
- Pay for a product/service, but a different product/service delivered.
- Asked to pay extra for superior product placement.
- Different pricing for same product/service depending on perceived status.

- Same law is swiftly applied in some instances, but very slowly or not at all in other instances of the same offence.
- Laws or regulations suddenly change and are applied to past events that were previously legal.

Corrupt practices or not? On the surface many readers will point to these as examples of corruption. Dig more deeply and the conclusion is not so clear. Let us go through them again.

Extra payment for special service: We do this every day with priority paid postage and delivery services, when we use a platinum credit card or the American Express concierge service to get priority seats and booking at events. Tip the restaurant concierge for the special table and for the attentive service. These are all so everyday that it doesn't feel corrupt, yet here is a payment that goes into an individual's pocket for a service delivered as part of his employment.

Asked to pay for 'special' service but service not delivered: Courier companies charge for express service delivery, but exclude certain areas. Despite the exclusion you still pay the full cost for this 'special' service. Payment for extra leg room seats on airlines represent a customer preference and not an airline obligation to provide the special service. Refunds are not available when the service is not delivered.

Pay for a product/service, but a different product/service delivered: This is a common embezzlement practised by governments. A levy or tax is imposed for a specific purpose but the bulk of funds raised disappear into general revenue. The intended beneficiary of these extra funds remains underfunded. Taxes on fuel or vehicle registration to fund road infrastructure are a common example where funds raised are only used in part for the intended purpose.

Asked to pay extra for superior product placement: Companies willingly pay for page premiums in advertising. Companies routinely pay for shelf space and shelf placement in supermarkets and chain stores.

Different pricing for same product/service depending on perceived status: One of the most dangerous questions you can ask on an airplane is how much the person beside you paid for their seat. There are a wide variety of pricing options depending on who you are and how you booked, but you all end up on the same flight and sitting in economy class. Airlines offer cheaper return flights from point A to B than the cost of the same return flight from B to A.

Same law is swiftly applied in some instances, but not in other instances of the same offence: The disproportionate number of non-Caucasians in American jails is a product of more than just social disadvantage. Numerous studies have shown how race affects the application of the law and the apprehension of suspects. The 2020 Black Lives Matter movement highlighted these issues.

Laws or regulations suddenly change and are applied to past events that were previously legal: In some countries, such as Australia, this has become so prevalent that it heightens concerns of sovereign risk. Some changes reach back a decade, imposing unexpected burdens on companies and individuals who complied with the law as it was at the time.

When these examples are placed in a Chinese context, we are quick to assume they are corrupt. Put them into our home context and they become normal business practices. Corruption does exist in China, but do not confuse every different business practice with corruption. Taking the high moral ground is a dangerous position when businesses routinely use similar practices in their home country.

It is exceptionally unwise to dismiss President Xi's Tiger and Flies anti-corruption campaign as primarily aimed at eliminating political opponents. The campaign has had a profound impact on the way business is done and in clamping down on petty corruption. Social media 'human flesh' searches have broadened the scope and effectiveness of calling out corruption.

The reliance on relationships as a foundation of reliable business may appear to lend itself more easily to concepts of corruption but it is not necessarily so. The corrupt and the venal exist in all societies, but so too do the honest and the ethical. You choose who you want to do business with and you bear the consequences of your choice.

What we think we know about China is most often inaccurate because it is based on a lifetime's unconscious accumulation of outdated myths and clichés. It is not just you and me. Sophisticated Western companies like News Ltd and Google can make mistakes of legendary proportions because their thinking is based on the same misconceptions. Our challenge is not to let these myths prevent us from doing better business in China.

## CHINA BUSINESS BITE

Myths and clichés have an origin in reality but they are often outdated. Be wary of the unconscious influence of these outdated concepts on your thinking. Good friendships are the foundation of sustainable China business and they require work to maintain. Don't confuse real corruption with business practices that are common in your home country but implemented slightly differently in China.

# CHAPTER 35

# INWARD LOOKING OUT

One of the most enduring myths is the idea that China is inward-looking and it needs opening up, preferably with the guidance of a benevolent West. We are here to help and you will become so much better if you adopt our ideas of democracy, of individualism and modern financial capitalism with its financial engineering. This idea was so pervasive at the turn of the 19th century that many Chinese came to accept its accuracy, including founding President of the Republic of China, Sun Yat-sen, who, like thousands of others, studied overseas.

In modern times there is both a conceit and condescension in this approach that does not go unrecognised in China. When China refuses to fully accept these benevolent offers the conversation takes a nastier turn. President Trump and his advisors are bitterly disappointed that China has not become more liberal as its prosperity increased. Their refusal is cast as part of a long history of China's inward-looking governance.

Myths are powerful in shaping our perceptions. Common and simplistic myths are usually easily dismissed as irrelevant, but some myths become more deeply, and dangerously entrenched. They have become so integrated with our thinking that we do not consider them as myths and we come to accept them as a short-hand for reality.

A museum exhibition on the discovery and restoration of a 9th century Tang Dynasty shipwreck smashed a few myths that had clouded my thinking about China even after having worked in China for more than a decade. These included:

The idea that the silk road was an intermittent and almost accidental trade route delivering an inconsistent dribble of trade between China and Europe. In fact, it was a regular, actively managed logistical link designed to feed foreign export markets with products specifically tailored for individual market segments.

The idea that factory mass production of identical items began in Britain or America. This treasure ship was full of mass produced, identical bowls and products destined for tables in Europe and elsewhere.

The idea that China can only imitate and not innovate. The use of the Chinese invention of gunpowder for fireworks rather than cannons is an extension of this myth of China's inability to innovate. These Tang dynasty export products were specifically created for export markets with designs unpopular in China, but much admired, and later imitated, in the West. This was a deliberately constructed export economy in the 9th century, at a time when we describe Europe as living in the Dark Ages.

The idea that China was essentially a collection of isolated provinces only technically united during the Tang dynasty. These trade export goods were sourced from multiple kilns spread across the width and breadth of China. This is a sophisticated domestic web of logistics, infrastructure and supply feeding into an equally sophisticated web of international logistics using land and sea resources.

The Tang Dynasty is rightly famous for its culture and classic poetry. It is rarely recognised for its pre-eminence in industrial production, logistics and its export economy. So why do we continue to accept this mythical image of a China cowering behind closed doors, unwelcoming of ideas from the West? Much of our modern thinking is based on myths deliberately created to justify war with China.

As a result of an intense propaganda campaign waged by hired writers in the letters pages of British newspapers to justify the outbreak of the first Opium War in 1830, it became fashionable to describe Qing China as stagnant, closed to the Western world, and not open to new ideas. Later it was characterised as a rogue state that refused to play by the new rules of free trade adopted by England and America. Even today this has a familiar ring. This propaganda ignored the reality that

Qing China was a vast, multi-ethnic empire with a voracious appetite for foreign languages, ideas and trade.

The Yuan Ming Yuan palace was destroyed by French and British troops on the orders of Lord Elgin. Captain, later General, Gordon of Khartoum fame, wrote: "You can scarcely imagine the beauty and magnificence of the places we burnt" and he regretted that "we were so pressed for time, that we could not plunder them carefully". Yuan Ming Yuan was a Chinese tribute to the most modern advances found in Europe and England. The ruins have been preserved and a visit gives some idea of the degree of European influence in design and architecture.

Many of us, and many of our political leaders, still accept one or both of these versions of Chinese history. China is a closed state that must learn to enjoy the benefits of opening up to Western ideas, or it is a rogue state that does not play by the rules of free trade. It is possible for some commentators to simultaneously accept both of these myths.

This myth of an inward-looking China is a puff of ignorance easily dispelled in any Chinese bookshop. As an author, I like to know what my competition is doing so I regularly spend some time browsing Chinese language bookstores in Beijing and Shanghai. Five of my financial market books are available in China in translation. One of my favourite haunts is the aptly named Paper Tiger bookshop in Haidian, Beijing.

Several years ago, the shelves in my preferred browsing section were an uneven mix of local books and foreign translations. The foreign translations dominated both shelf space and premium pricing. Our cultural arrogance leads us to the conclusion that this is because Chinese writers have little to say on financial markets. Nothing could be further from the truth. Books written by Chinese traders were as advanced and sophisticated as those written by American authors. The range of Chinese authors reflected the same range found in Western authors writing on this subject.

There was one important difference in this Beijing bookstore when compared to a similar non-fiction section in an American or London bookstore. Other than novels, these Western bookstores carry very few translated works by Chinese authors. Western publishers do not see a market for these non-fiction translations. Without these technical and research books on shelves, Western readers believe there is nothing of value written in this area by Chinese authors because no translated books are available. This is the most significant gap in our thinking.

We often make a false assumption when we cannot read Chinese. It means we are unaware of the advances being made until they are translated. And what is translated is often one generation behind the cutting edge of thinking and development. This underestimation is the major challenge to understanding the business opportunities and the level of competition in China. We create our own myths through ignorance.

The Paper Tiger bookshop in Haidian is not the preserve of academics and specialists. It is a small bookstore chain, and its customers are ordinary people. The availability of translated works is not restricted to experts and professionals.

The books displayed on shelves reflect consumer demand and interest. Our interest in China has grown, but this has not always been matched in an increase in understanding. In Singapore, entire bookshelves are dedicated to contemporary Chinese politics, business and economics. China is not an unknown country. It is of intense interest to Americans and shelves are dominated by American analysis of China. Some feed on fear whilst others welcome the competition and some try to explain what can be learned from China.

Unlike a Chinese bookstore, only a handful of Chinese business and reference books are available in translation. It means we are not in touch with the diversity of modern Chinese thinking in the same way that the Chinese are in touch with the diversity of Western thinking via a wide range of translated works. The paucity of translated books available in this area impacts on, and reflects the quality of debate and understanding within the broader Western community. It suggests our understanding of our largest trading partner is at best very shallow, and at worst, seriously out of touch with the rapidly developing and changing economic and political environment.

Part of that change includes the greatest human migration seen since the Industrial Revolution. This is an apparently easy concept to grasp in abstract, or vicariously through books including *Factory Girls, Northern Girls* and others. They focus on the exploitation of the rural poor and hopefuls, feeding into the mill of another cliché that left unchallenged, can overpower the broader reality on the ground.

China is a nation of domestic migrants. I was reminded of this in both Guangzhou and again in Shanghai. It started with a conversation with the assistant manager in a Guangzhou hotel. He had a strong northern accent and I asked where he was from. He confirmed his home town was Harbin in Northeast China. Talking to senior hotel staff in Guangzhou revealed people from Nanjing, Harbin, Xi'an and Shenyang. Hotel staff in Shanghai originally came from Beijing, Dalian and Tianjin. Conversations with business people and officials revealed a similar spread of diverse hometowns.

We are all familiar with the rapid growth of Shanghai, Shenzhen, Beijing and almost any other city in the eastern areas of China you care to name. This awareness is not always coupled with the next and obvious conclusion. This massive urbanisation is a product of an equally massive displacement of people. This is a mass internal migration greater than that experienced during the Industrial Revolution in Europe.

We tend to think of this as low-class labourers moving to the cities in search of work. The plight of poor rural workers living in Shanghai and elsewhere without residence permits has featured regularly in the foreign media. We have a vague impression the teeming workers on the construction sites are from the countryside although we do not pause to wonder where they are living.

There is no denying the mass migration of less skilled labour to the cities in search of work. What we are less aware of is the mass migration of skilled workers to cities and locations far from their home towns. China has more than six million university graduates each year and few of them will return to their home towns. Many will travel to new cities picking up jobs they have applied for and won. This is not speculative travel in the hope of getting a job. This is planned movement, taking geographical steps in a well thought out and defined career path.

These are not people living in hastily constructed workers quarters on the edge of a construction site. These are established and increasingly wealthy middle-class migrants owning apartments and cars and aspiring to move into better apartment with better jobs, possibly in another city. We cannot ignore the desperation of the unskilled migrant, but we should not let this cliché obscure other aspects of this movement.

This movement gives a dynamism to China. This population shift creates a frontier mentality that makes people more open to new ideas and new thinking. It takes courage, not desperation, to move from one substantial city to another. With that courage comes a commitment to improvement and progress because where you are now has to be better than where you were before.

By virtue of the speed and size of change, China must be aware of its internal developments but it continues to look outwards to source the seeds of continual improvement. This is a continuation of a heritage extending back to the Tang dynasty. China is a well-established trading nation ready and willing to do business in goods, services and ideas.

## CHINA BUSINESS BITE

China welcomes new ideas, but the focus is on exploring the best of those ideas to improve conditions in China. Sometimes this may involve direct substitution but more often it requires creative adaptation.

# Chapter 36

## CAN YOU BE THE ONE?

Fans of the brutal Chinese dating show **If You Are the One** will have some idea of the requirements of the young women on it when it comes to assessing prospective dates. Just having money, or an apartment and a car is not enough. As I was told in Shanghai, the definition of true love is when a woman agrees to meet with a man who has an apartment in Pudong, as this is considered very much a less prestigious area of Shanghai.

But the translation of **If You Are the One** is not quite correct. The name of the show 非诚勿扰 (*fei cheng wu rao*) is better translated as **Please Do Not Disturb Me Unless You Are Sincere**. The difference in translation is important in several ways. It highlights the importance of the quality of translation and interpretation to capture the correct meaning. And the dating show reveals some significant aspects that can be applied to business dating in China.

The dating show is brutal and so is business dating in China. In Shanghai, I was asked to talk with an Australian SME which is thinking of expanding into China. Like some of the men on **If You Are the One**, the staff of the SME was very confident of its appeal. They have an established brand in Australia and they believe their service will be appealing to Chinese customers. Although by their standards they are a well-established and reasonably sized SME, this does not transfer well in the Chinese environment.

Their entire staff size is the equivalent of the full staff in a small branch office of a Chinese company in a tier 4 city. It's a little bit like having an apartment in Pudong because it's going to require true love for a much larger Chinese partner to develop co-operation with this smaller SME.

The task is not impossible, but the way the SME was going about attracting the interest of a co-operation partner and then developing a co-operation agreement was very different from the way the SME had imagined. Like the male contestants on the dating show, its worth is not self-evident and the features the staff think are of value may be of little interest to the prospective partner.

As Wu Zhengzhen told one suitor on the dating show, it's not about what you can offer. It's about understanding what the prospective partner wants. In business this means understanding how you can contribute to the Chinese partner because it is them who are doing you a favour by working with a much much smaller company like yours. It means framing your proposal in a framework that is familiar to the Chinese partner and to Chinese political priorities including the Belt and Road Initiative.

Rather than rush into a proposal, it's better to spend time understanding the market environment before entering the dating scene. Only then is everything possible.

The day before the historic change in Chinese leadership was a cold winter's day in Beijing. Heavy snow had fallen a few days earlier. The Australian Cabinet Minister I was supporting had some free time due to a cancelled meeting. He wanted to see Tiananmen Square and walk in the Forbidden City. The official advice was that none of this was possible due to the expected security clampdown.

I escorted the Minister into a plain-plated black Audi and the driver took us around Tiananmen Square, driving directly past the Chinese parliament building, slowing for photographs. The Minister took a look at the hour-long line of mainly foreigners and visitors queuing for tickets for entry into the Forbidden City. As this was an unofficial tour, it would not be possible to jump the line and the Minister was resigned to missing the opportunity to visit.

I used the Chinese approach. There is always a side door solution for any problem. In this case I directed the driver to go to Dongmen — the east gate. The driver dropped us at the east gate and we walked along the side of the Forbidden City wall with the bitter cold wind blowing across the moat. We stood in line for two minutes, collected tickets and were inside the Forbidden City within eight minutes. Local knowledge provides legitimate short cuts so you can go where the Chinese go.

The tourists attack the Forbidden City at the front gate. Foreign business often attacks China business by seeking entry through the front gate. You can attempt to storm the gates but in return you can expect to be repelled — and exploited. The full-frontal approach sets you up as an enemy or a willing victim.

It's most clearly seen in companies that go to China to take advantage of cheap labour and cheap production costs. The factory girls in Shenzhen, Guangzhou, Shanghai, and a multitude of other cities are not stupid. They look at the shoes and bags they are producing. They look at the end result of their labours in the high-end shops in Shanghai and note the prices. They compare the asking price to the levels of wages they are paid. This exploitation gap puts out the welcome mat for counterfeiters.

According to some commentators, the Chinese steal your ideas, your products, your copyright, your intellectual property. It's a monotonous litany of excuses for Western business failure from those who cannot understand that exploitation is not a path to sustainable business success. The American publishing industry was founded on exploiting books pirated from England and published without regard to English copyright. It was only as America began to produce its own authors that the American publishing industry discovered the benefits of rigorously enforced copyright.

Exploitation in the age of the internet is even less viable. It was said in the 1960s that the refrigerator became a symbol of revolution because it showed the third world what the first world enjoyed. In the 21st century the internet provides rapid confirmation of exploitation. So, some people reason, producing a cheaper knock-off, perhaps using the same production process and production line, reflects a true capitalist competitive pressure.

My business in China is built entirely around intellectual property. I cannot protect it successfully in China, but my Chinese partners can protect it. They choose to do so because my business success is part of their business success. Part of their profitable outcome depends on protecting my intellectual property. Our objectives are the same.

My friend Nannan works very hard. Often, I will wish her a happy weekend. She replies, 一样, 一样. *Yi yang, yi yang,* same same.

Ultimately, you get out of your China business what you sincerely put into your China business, and often more than you expect. It is same same. Exploiters are in turn exploited. Sincere friends are rewarded in ways that go well beyond any monetary return. There is always a side gate alternative to the full-frontal assault. The Manchu found the side gate at Shanhai Pass in 1644 and founded the Qing Dynasty. Your SME business may not be of the same size, but the methods are the same.

## CHINA BUSINESS BITE

This is Chapter 36, and famously the last of the 36 strategies of the Chinese is to run away. This book is designed to show you how to run away from your preconceptions so you can prosper and enjoy China with fresh eyes and perspectives.

# ABOUT THE AUTHOR

**Daryl Guppy** is the founder and CEO of Guppytraders.com, an international financial market education and training organisation with offices in Darwin, Singapore and Beijing. Daryl Guppy has decades of experience working in China business relationships. He is a national board member of the Australia China Business Council and the Australian representative on the Silk Road Chambers of International Commerce. He has worked with the Chief Ministers' Department of the Northern Territory (NT), Australia and with other senior NT Ministers on China matters.

He is an invited speaker at ASEAN and APEC conferences in China, and has spoken on Belt and Road Initiative (New Silk Road) policies in China, Singapore and Australia. He appears frequently on CNBC Asia and China's CGTN business news. He writes weekly columns for *The Edge*, *China Daily* and *Shanghai Security News*, *CGTN Digital* and a CNBC.com column — Charting Asia. He has authored nine books on financial market, including *Trend Trading and The 36 Strategies of the Chinese for Financial Traders*.

Printed in the United States
by Baker & Taylor Publisher Services